THE COAST TO COAST CYCLE ROUTE

WHITEHAVEN OR WORKINGTON TO TYNEMOUTH OR SUNDERLAND

By Carl McKeating and Rachel Crolla

JUNIPER HOUSE, MURLEY MOSS,
OXENHOLME ROAD, KENDAL, CUMBRIA LA9 7RL
www.cicerone.co.uk

© Carl McKeating and Rachel Crolla 2023
First edition 2023
ISBN: 978 1 78631 118 4

Printed in India by Replika Press Pvt Ltd using responsibly sourced paper.
A catalogue record for this book is available from the British Library.
All photographs are by the authors unless otherwise stated.

Route mapping by Lovell Johns www.lovelljohns.com
Contains OpenStreetMap.org data © OpenStreetMap
contributors, CC-BY-SA. NASA relief data courtesy of ESRI

This book is dedicated to Dave Crolla – he loved this route and returned to it many times.

Updates to this guide

While every effort is made by our authors to ensure the accuracy of guidebooks as they go to print, changes can occur during the lifetime of an edition. Any updates that we know of for this guide will be on the Cicerone website (www.cicerone.co.uk/1118/updates), so please check before planning your trip. We also advise that you check information about such things as transport, accommodation and shops locally. Even rights of way can be altered over time.

We are always grateful for information about any discrepancies between a guidebook and the facts on the ground, sent by email to updates@cicerone.co.uk or by post to Cicerone, Juniper House, Murley Moss, Oxenholme Road, Kendal, LA9 7RL.

Register your book: To sign up to receive free updates, special offers and GPX files where available, register your book at www.cicerone.co.uk.

Front cover: Between Leadgate and Hartside Top on the hilly middle section of the C2C (Day 2)

CONTENTS

Ride planner.. 5
Route summary tables 6

INTRODUCTION 11
Why choose the C2C? 12
How tough is the ride? 13
How many days? 16
Where to start and where to end................................... 19
West to east or east to west? 20
What kind of bicycle? 21
Unsurfaced off-road options 23
Getting there and back 25
Where to stay 27
Before setting off on your bike 28
Equipment 28
Carrying your gear 29
What to wear 30
Maps and apps 30
Signage... 31
Using this guide 32

THE C2C 33
Day 1   Whitehaven to Greystoke 34
Day 1A   Workington to Greystoke 54
Day 2   Greystoke to Allenheads 63
Day 3   Allenheads to Tynemouth 81
Day 3A   Allenheads to Sunderland 104

Appendix A   Accommodation.................................... 114
Appendix B   Bike shops and other useful contacts 121

Passing Ribton House just before Great Broughton (Stage 1A)

Acknowledgements

The authors would like to thank Scott Barnett for being such an entertaining companion during their first C2C outing in 2002 and for his support with this book. Thanks to the 'Brownlee Sisters' – Harriet Truss, Louise Robinson and Romily Thistlethwaite for joining Rachel on yet another crossing. Thanks also to 'Team Sumo' – Dave Crolla, Andy Midgely and Jim Schofield – whose perennial returns to the ride gave us a sense of its history and appeal. As ever, thanks to our two daughters, Heather and Rosa, for their continued enthusiasm, additional photography and patience throughout the project.

Note on mapping

The base maps onto which the authors have charted the routes in this guide are derived from publicly available data rather than from an official mapping agency. They have been checked by the authors.

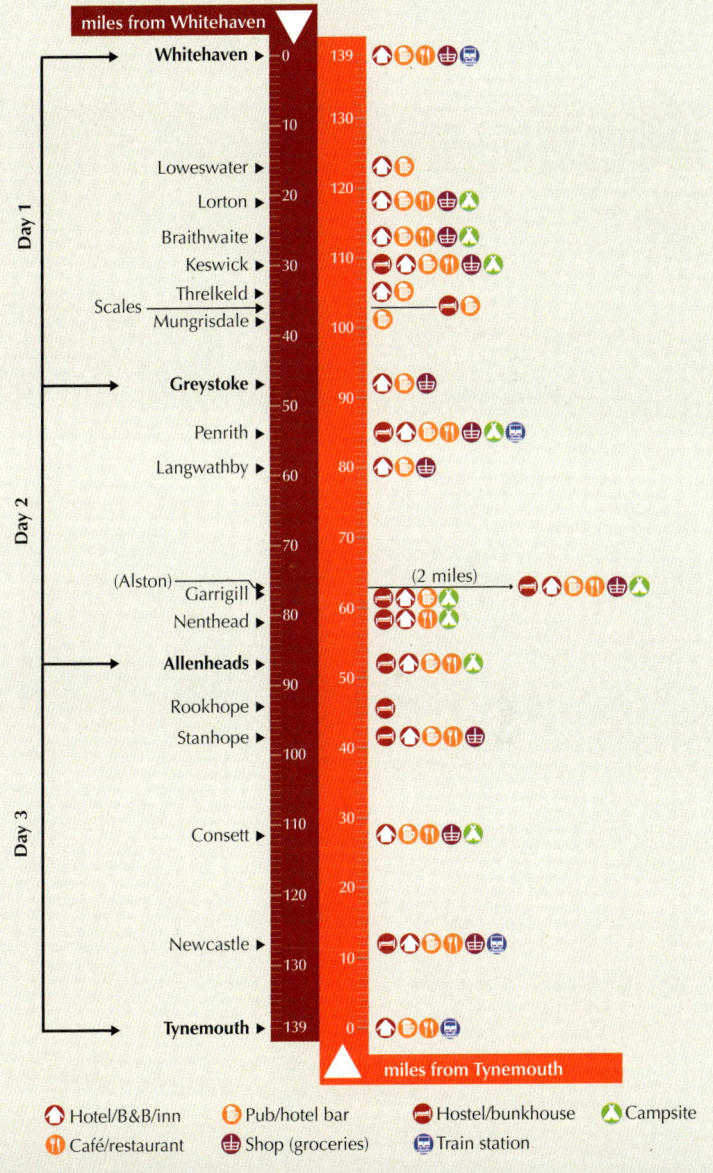

The Coast to Coast Cycle Route

ROUTE SUMMARY TABLES

C2C Whitehaven to Tynemouth/Sunderland three-day itinerary					
	Start	**Finish**	**Distance**	**Ascent**	**Page**
Day 1	Whitehaven (NX 969 182)	Greystoke (NY 440 309)	47 miles (76km)	1251m	34
Day 2	Greystoke (NY 440 309)	Allenheads (NY 860 453)	40 miles (65km)	1533m	63
Day 3	Allenheads (NY 860 453)	Tynemouth (NZ 374 691)	52 miles (83km)	845m	81
Day 3	Allenheads (NY 860 453)	Sunderland (NZ 408 589)	49 miles (79km)	822m	104
Total	**Whitehaven (NX 969 182)**	**Tynemouth (NZ 374 691) or Sunderland (NZ 408 589)**	**139 miles (224km) or 137 miles (220km)**	3629m or 3606m	

C2C Whitehaven to Tynemouth/Sunderland four-day itinerary					
	Start	**Finish**	**Distance**	**Ascent (approx)**	**Page**
Day 1	Whitehaven (NX 969 182)	Threlkeld (NY 320 254)	35 miles (56km)	910m	34
Day 2	Threlkeld (NY 320 254)	Garrigill (NY 745 416)	43 miles (70km)	1301m	46
Day 3	Garrigill (NY 745 416)	Parkhead (NZ 003 432)	23 miles (37km)	1087m	74
Day 4	Parkhead (NZ 003 432)	Tynemouth (NZ 374 691)	38 miles (61km)	331m	86
Day 4	Parkhead (NZ 003 432)	Sunderland (NZ 408 589)	36 miles (58km)	308m	86
Total	**Whitehaven (NX 969 182)**	**Tynemouth (NZ 374 691) or Sunderland (NZ 408 589)**	**139 miles (224km) or 137 miles (220km)**	3629m or 3606m	

ROUTE SUMMARY TABLES

C2C Workington to Tynemouth/Sunderland three-day itinerary

	Start	Finish	Distance	Ascent	Page
Day 1	Workington (NX 982 297)	Greystoke (NY 440 309)	44 miles (71km)	1191m	54
Day 2	Greystoke (NY 440 309)	Allenheads (NY 860 453)	40 miles (65km)	1533m	63
Day 3	Allenheads (NY 860 453)	Tynemouth (NZ 374 691)	52 miles (83km)	845m	81
Day 3	Allenheads (NY 860 453)	Sunderland (NZ 408 589)	49 miles (79km)	822m	104
Total	**Workington (NX 982 297)**	**Tynemouth (NZ 374 691) or Sunderland (NZ 408 589)**	**136 miles (219km) or 134 miles (216km)**	**3569m or 3546m**	

C2C Workington to Tynemouth/Sunderland four-day itinerary

	Start	Finish	Distance	Ascent (approx)	Page
Day 1	Workington (NX 982 297)	Threlkeld (NY 320 254)	32 miles (51km)	850m	54
Day 2	Threlkeld (NY 320 254)	Langwathby (NY 567 337)	25 miles (40km)	539m	46
Day 3	Langwathby (NY 567 337)	Rookhope (NY 939 429)	34 miles (55km)	1489m	68
Day 4	Rookhope (NY 939 429)	Tynemouth (NZ 374 691)	45 miles (72km)	691m	83
Day 4	Rookhope (NY 939 429)	Sunderland (NZ 408 589)	42 miles (68km)	668m	83
Total	**Workington (NX 982 297)**	**Tynemouth (NZ 374 691) or Sunderland (NZ 408 589)**	**136 miles (219km) or 134 miles (216km)**	**3569m or 3546m**	

The Coast to Coast Cycle Route

C2C Whitehaven to Tynemouth/Sunderland two-day itinerary

	Start	Finish	Distance	Ascent	Page
Day 1	Whitehaven (NX 969 182)	Garrigill (NY 745 416)	78 miles (126km)	2211m	34
Day 2	Garrigill (NY 745 416)	Tynemouth (NZ 374 691)	61 miles (98km)	1418m	74
Day 2	Garrigill (NY 745 416)	Sunderland (NZ 408 589)	58 miles (94km)	1395m	74
Total	**Whitehaven (NX 969 182)**	**Tynemouth (NZ 374 691) or Sunderland (NZ 408 589)**	**139 miles (224km) or 137 miles (220km)**	**3629m or 3606m**	

C2C Workington to Tynemouth/Sunderland two-day itinerary

	Start	Finish	Distance	Ascent	
Day 1	Workington (NX 982 297)	Garrigill (NY 745 416)	75 miles (120km)	2151m	54
Day 2	Garrigill (NY 745 416)	Tynemouth (NZ374 691)	61 miles (98km)	1418m	74
Day 2	Garrigill (NY 745 416)	Sunderland (NZ 408 589)	59 miles (95km)	1395m	74
Total	**Workington (NX 982 297)**	**Tynemouth (NZ 374 691) or Sunderland (NZ 408 589)**	**136 miles (219km) or 134 miles (216km)**	**3569m or 3546m**	

Passing Loweswater and its distinctive guardian, Mellbreak (Stage 1)

Crossing Wainford Bridge on the approach to Allenheads (Stage 2)

INTRODUCTION

Passing Ennerdale Water with Pillar in the distance (Stage 1)

Arcing its way from Irish Sea to North Sea across an absorbing and beautiful swathe of northern England, the 139-mile Sea to Sea Cycle Route (or 'C2C') is an essential rite of passage for cycle enthusiasts. Comfortably Britain's most popular cycling challenge, since its inception in 1994 it has proved to be the mother of Sustrans' ever-burgeoning family of tours. The many cyclists that return to it year after year are testament to its enduring success. Whether solo or in a group, riders tend to discover a supportive camaraderie while cycling along the course or resting in tearoom stops and at overnight accommodation. Unquestionably, the C2C remains *the* cycle tour against which all other British tours are compared: veterans will give knowing nods about its merits and challenges, while no cycle tour discussion would ever be complete without references to it.

Adopting a west–east direction to take advantage of prevailing westerly winds, the route strikes eastwards from the Cumbrian coast stitching together the lakes and mountains of the northern Lake District to create a picturesque collage. Here, cyclists weave their way, soaring upwards and gliding downwards as the lakes of Ennerdale Water, Loweswater, Crummock Water, Bassenthwaite and Derwent Water find vertiginous guardians in the mountains of Pillar, Grasmoor, Hopegill Head, Catbells, Skiddaw and Blencathra.

THE COAST TO COAST CYCLE ROUTE

Beyond the Lake District, the route bridges across the verdant Eden Valley – via Penrith – and ventures into the wild beauty of the lesser-known northern Pennines. Overlapping fells now briefly capture cyclists in steep-sided land-that-time-forgot valleys, before challenging escapes gain hilltops and high moorlands that reward endurance and perseverance with scenes of sublime wuthering vastness. The challenging traverse of the spine of England culminates at the remote Parkhead Station – a relic of an improbable upland mining railway. From Parkhead, the route commences a delightfully elongated descent towards the North Sea, wending its way along more than thirty miles of adapted former rail lines and cycle paths to the coast.

In many ways, the C2C is an umbrella route. It has a series of options that pose a few quandaries to the tourer even before setting out. The choice of where to start (Whitehaven or Workington) and finish (Tynemouth or Sunderland) requires a spot of contemplation. Whitehaven is the more popular of the two starts, while Tynemouth is the more popular of the two finishes. Reflecting this, they feature in our primary route description. Conversely, Workington and Sunderland, which both have their individual merits, are included as fully described alternatives (see Where to start and where to end).

While the ride is more commonly tackled by cyclists on road bikes, the route nonetheless presents a series of alternative unsurfaced off-road options that need consideration. Although a couple of these were originally intended as the primary route line (and in the case of the bone-jangling off-road descent of Whinlatter, remain so) the majority tend to be ignored in favour of good road options. However, some – such as the climb via Bolts Law standing engine to Parkhead – present truly impressive riding and may tip the balance away from road bikes. Other alternative off-road variations always seemed like an afterthought by Sustrans. These have, over the years, tended only to be tackled by masochists. To help planning before setting out, refer to the Unsurfaced off-road options and What kind of bicycle sections of this introduction.

WHY CHOOSE THE C2C?

Every cyclist in Britain should do the C2C at least once. As the original coast-to-coast ride, it is deservedly well-known and popular. Initially, the designers envisaged C2C completists collecting a series of 6 special stamps on route that enabled a commemorative T-shirt to be acquired, but this idea seems to have fallen out of favour; this is a special route that needs no gimmicks to promote it.

With its simple yet romantic premise of crossing the country from one sea to another, the route has come to be seen as the classic short British cycle tour. Where less-confident

At 457m, Nenthead is one of the highest villages in England (Stage 2)

cyclists might choose the slightly easier Hadrian's Cycleway or Way of the Roses coast to coast routes, the C2C is nonetheless an achievable goal for most, and the advent of e-bikes has broadened its accessibility. More than any other, the C2C sees a phenomenal number of repeat riders; its multiple route options, good signage and links to other routes help explain this. Over the years a mini economy has grown up around providing services for the thousands of C2C cyclists who complete the route each year. Transport companies abound and, while Covid closures forced many amenities on route to shut down, doing the C2C is a great way to support local businesses in parts of the country where it really matters – what better excuse to make numerous café stops!

HOW TOUGH IS THE RIDE?

The C2C offers a good balance of challenge over a three-day tour and is an attainable goal for most regular cyclists. If you can comfortably ride 40 miles with 1000m of ascent and still clamber back onto your saddle the next day, then you will be more than able to tackle the three-day itinerary. A west–east C2C works well insofar as once the challenging Pennines are finally crossed and the remote Parkhead Station is reached, the remaining 37 miles or so to Tynemouth or 35 miles to Sunderland are nearly all either downhill or flat – a tremendous incentive and boost to any riders who are 'hilled-out'.

The C2C involves some tough climbing when compared with similar Sustrans three-day coast-to-coast tours. It has roughly 1400m more ascent than Hadrian's Cycleway, and 825m more ascent than the Way of the Roses. Fortunately, this extra climbing is offset by a reduced distance: the C2C is shorter than the Way of the Roses and Hadrian's Cycleway by 33 and 37 miles respectively. The following ascent data is based on the present OS mapping tool.

- Coast to Coast 139 miles, 3629m ascent, standard tour 3 days
- Way of the Roses 170 miles, 2823m ascent, standard tour 3 days
- Hadrian's Cycleway 174 miles, 2109m ascent, standard tour 3 days
- Reivers Route, 173 miles, 3780m ascent, standard tour 4 days
- Yorkshire Dales Cycleway 133 miles, 4306m ascent, standard tour 3 days

The climbs

Day 1

On Day 1, crossing the Lake District is an unsurprisingly fairly hilly affair. Nonetheless, it is not remotely as challenging as might be expected and certainly not as challenging as it could have been made. Riders are confronted with one truly daunting big climb – the ascent of **Whinlatter Pass** (258m height gain). While Whinlatter is a great climb and a good challenge, it is the tamest and least gruelling of the big Lakeland passes. Almost all find it enjoyable, while the views of Skiddaw that appear on cresting the pass amply repay all the effort involved in getting there.

Day 2

Day 2 of the C2C is, simply put, a beast. Hills abound – if you do not like them, you may regret not opting for Norfolk or Holland. Yet these grand ascents are what give the route its character and legendary status. The day has a series of testing and memorable climbs, although two in particular will live long in the memory. **Hartside Top** (575m, 383m height gain) is one of the most protracted and impressive ascents in Great Britain. Because its steepest moments barely touch 1 in 5, on a cool, still day it is possible to settle into a steady rhythm and really soak up the sense of climbing into the high Pennines. Nonetheless, for many riders the climb proves to be the most psychologically and physically challenging of the hills on the C2C. Its long nature is impressed upon every cog spin by the 'still-that-far-away!' top being in sight for the majority of the climb. Likewise, because the treeless Hartside road snakes towards the sky, riders are exposed to the elements and will find any moments of hoped-for wind assistance are likely to be balanced by unwelcome moments of wind opposition.

Conversely, the Garrigill climb (599m) over **Flinty Fell** (268m height gain) is very much a direct test-piece. Its initial escape from the valley floor serves up a delightfully brutish 1 in 4.

This sees many tourers resort to bike-pushing. Nonetheless, it is a beast quickly tamed and the determined will be pleased to find that after the initial short struggle, the gradient eases substantially and the climb relaxes into a pleasant if elongated affair. Two further substantial climbs intercede between Nenthead and Allenheads. The first is the high point of the C2C at a dizzying 609m on **Black Hill** (152m height gain). This point is only 150m above Nenthead and although initially hard up to a left turn, most will settle into a good rhythm and achieve the summit on the fifth-highest road in England with relative ease. After dropping down just over 100m from Black Hill, the final climb of the day over **Killhope Law** (586m, 81m height gain) is not so tough – assuming riders have anything left in the legs, that is.

Day 3
Day 3 serves up three more highly rewarding hills before giving way to easy terrain. The first challenge is a long and extremely pleasant **climb from Allenheads** (130m height gain) which includes a set of forested switchbacks that give a hint of the alpine before open moorland leads to a lofty beehive-shaped 'currick' (cairn) guarding the entrance to Rookhope Dale. The day's second big climb is an elegant if challenging affair that makes great use of a wonderful minor road over **Coal Crow Hill** (115m height gain) to Stanhope. The final big climb of the C2C is the notorious **Crawleyside Bank** (254m height gain) between Stanhope and Parkhead Station. This is no toy. It peaks with a fairly long passage of 1 in 5 and considerable graft is required to overcome this monster ascent.

Having accomplished the long climb of Hartside (Stage 2)

On the superbly secluded Mungrisdale road (Stage 1)

HOW MANY DAYS?

The majority of cyclists opt to ride the C2C in three days and do so mostly choosing the road and well-surfaced traffic-free options described as the primary route in this book. Cyclists on gravel bikes or similar, who take some of the off-road options, will spend longer in the saddle, but can still consider a three-day itinerary. Three days generally works well for relatively fit regular cyclists who can manage the hills. Three days allows for less than 50 miles of cycling on average each day; and it gives enough slack to allow for punctures, sociable lunches and evening pub visits. A three-day trip also allows some cyclists time to travel to and from the beginning and end of the route, although an overnight stay at one or both ends is also very common. The three-day ride has a first day which becomes hillier in the afternoon, a second day that is very hilly and, finally, a third day with three hills up front in the morning, followed by the relief of a very easy afternoon.

The three-day itinerary can be adapted to suit individual needs. Although we have suggested stopping at Greystoke and Allenheads, cyclists who have travelled further to the start of the route might reasonably stop in Keswick and have a shorter first day – yet this can make the second day quite tough. Similarly, many three-day C2C riders choose a longer first day finishing in or around Penrith. Both Keswick and Penrith have the advantage of ample accommodation and food and drink options. The second

HOW MANY DAYS?

night on a three-day C2C ride might be spent anywhere from Nenthead to Parkhead, depending on how long a ride is planned on the last day. Bear in mind that accommodation in the Nenthead–Stanhope section of the route is not as plentiful and popular stop-offs in Allenheads are booked up well in advance on Saturday nights. The route summary tables should help with planning.

A four-day ride is also a good choice for those coming from further afield, cyclists completing their first tour or less confident about the hills, or heavily loaded cycle-campers, as well as those wanting to tackle all the unsurfaced off-road alternatives.

A great itinerary for a four-day crossing would be spending the nights in Keswick, Garrigill or Alston (off-route) and Parkhead Station.

Many fit cyclists, who ride regularly in hilly terrain and understand what is involved in northern hills, complete the C2C in two days. The Garrigill or Alston (off-route) area would be the ideal stop, although Nenthead also seems a popular place to aim for on this schedule. A stop in Garrigill balances both the distance and climbing of two roughly 70-mile stages. Bear in mind what you want to get out of doing the ride: a two-day C2C ride might be deemed a 'challenge' for many strong cyclists,

Whitehaven's Candlestick chimney and the Beacon from the harbour (Stage 1)

whereas a three-day ride could be a short cycling holiday with friends for those same people.

Taking five days is possible, particularly for families, but probably overkill and not particularly helpful: the many challenging hill climbs involved in the escapade will still need to be ridden.

An extensive accommodation list for all the above itineraries is in Appendix A.

THE ONE DAY C2C CHALLENGE RIDE

Over the years, the C2C has attracted many cyclists looking to complete the ride in one day. This can be fun for seasoned and well-prepared super-fit cyclists. It should be done for enjoyment or not at all. Riders wanting to look themselves in the mirror afterwards should cycle it properly; otherwise, why bother? To that end, there is no point spoiling the ride and turning it into an ugly experience by taking direct fast shortcuts such as adopting the A66 to cut out the six-gate digression to Mungrisdale.

In research for this book, one of the authors enjoyed doing the day ride solo and entirely unsupported. If riders must have a support vehicle, they should remember that the C2C is not all about them and ensure that support vehicles avoid driving the route and instead only meet up at limited designated stops. After all, this is not the Tour de France – other cyclists will not appreciate additional vehicles ploughing up and down minor roads marring the route.

Preparation is everything. If you are unfamiliar with the hills of northern England, it is worth pointing out that the challenge of this day ride is not the distance – it is the successiveness and severity of the climbing. It is not a challenge to be taken lightly. A final preparation ride to test viability is important and should ideally involve a route in similarly hilly terrain of at least 90 miles. This can be tricky for those cyclists from flatter parts of the UK. To a Welsh, Scottish or northern cyclist, Box Hill would be little more than a speed bump, so riders in flatter regions such as the south-east should consider a preparation ride of 180 miles to get a sense of the challenge that the northern hills will impart.

Both C2C starts and finishes are viable for a one day attempt. Choosing a hybrid or gravel bike to incorporate some of the unsurfaced off-road sections into a Day Challenge would be a very slow, extremely tough, but nonetheless possible option for indefatigable warriors. Such an enterprise would need careful planning and would benefit from long daylight hours.

WHERE TO START AND WHERE TO END

There is no easy answer to either of these questions. Both C2C starts and endings are 'official' options and, as many riders return to the route, they will find them a great opportunity to choose a different one to their previous outing. To reflect the more popular choices made by C2C riders, the primary description in this book begins in Whitehaven and ends in Tynemouth. That does not imply that the Whitehaven start is better than the Workington one or that Tynemouth makes for a better ending than Sunderland.

In many ways, the tranquil out-of-the-way setting of the Workington start point, with its beach and views of Scotland makes it a considerably better launchpad than Whitehaven's busy marina. Knowing the pleasant Whitehaven start very well before writing this book, the authors were surprised by the Workington start and actually preferred it. With the Workington start there is a much better sense of being at the sea.

Likewise, while the Workington option – which hardly brushes the town of Workington – cannot boast as many miles on reclaimed railway or the close-up scenes of Ennerdale, Loweswater, Grasmoor, Crummock Water and Mellbreak offered by the Whitehaven approach – it nonetheless provides brilliant and highly enjoyable riding that unfurls splendorous watercolour views of the north-eastern Lake District. Incorporating a tremendous, if circuitous, section through the brilliant Cockermouth also counts heavily in favour of the Workington start. The Workington option now meets the main route in the delightful village of Lorton at the foot of the classic Whinlatter ascent and is much better than its original incarnation that did not meet the Whitehaven start until Braithwaite. The Workington option is shorter by a negligible 3 – flattish – miles and has 60m less ascent, but takes almost exactly the same amount of time because it is less direct.

Again, our primary description reflects the fact that a higher proportion of cyclists are drawn to ending in Tynemouth. This might be because Newcastle upon Tyne, with its famous Tyne Bridge and Great North Run, is more well-known. Many will enjoy the vibrant atmosphere of the River Tyne waterfront, although those who prefer a calmer ride welcome the Sunderland option, which eventually follows the generally quiet north side of the Wear.

The Tynemouth ending of the C2C on the raised headland of the Spanish Battery with its nearby priory and castle allows great views, although a brief continuation to find the sea is needed. Yet somehow the Tynemouth finish does not quite match the climactic finality of rounding Sunderland's excellent River Wear path and marina to reach the seafront at the pleasant Roker beach, which has seen a lot of investment over the last thirty years

E-W on the Whinlatter pass with Skiddaw beyond (Stage 1)

and boasts a picturesque pier and lighthouse. In all, the Sunderland ending is negligibly shorter by 2 miles. However, the cycle paths on the Sunderland route are more meandering and less well-surfaced for road bikes. Both finishes end up taking roughly the same amount of time.

WEST TO EAST OR EAST TO WEST?

The C2C has signage that works in either direction. To take advantage of Britain's prevailing westerly winds, the route is best tackled west–east. This direction has the advantage of leaving a last thirty or so miles that are either downhill or flat. Additionally, a west–east crossing tends to favour cyclists with more elongated smooth descents than an east–west crossing. The descents from Hartside Top, Shivery Fell, the 'currick' above Allenheads and from Parkhead Station towards the sea, each make the most of any height gained.

Nonetheless, prevailing easterlies are not unheard of in Britain and the C2C is perfectly viable east to west. The main disadvantage east–west is that the ascent of Hartside in this direction involves 3 miles of slow climbing on an A Road which zips by in the opposite direction. The main advantage east–west is that views of the Lake District tend to be more spectacular and easier to soak up. While east–west cannot boast a finish with over thirty miles of downhill/flat terrain, it does culminate in 9 miles of gradual descent to the Irish Sea. In terms of hill climbing, both directions tend to balance themselves out: even the notorious ascent from Garrigill finds its equivalent on the opposite side of the hill with a 1 in 4 out of Nenthead. It is worth noting, however, that the unsurfaced off-road ascent of Whinlatter, if opted for, will almost certainly require significant bike-pushing. Conversely, the Old Coach Road is much easier east–west.

Notes on east–west options are given at the end of each day's description.

WHAT KIND OF BICYCLE?

The C2C was never intended to be a pure definitive route, but rather a base route with a variety of different options and alternatives which are all best suited to different types of bicycles. A version of the C2C is absolutely possible on whatever type of bike you have, however, careful reading of the Unsurfaced off-road options section in this introduction should help planning and bike selection.

Reflecting the increased popularity of road biking since the millennium, there is no doubt that a C2C route suited to **road bikes** is presently the most popular choice. The main route line we describe in this book is suitable for road bikes. Absolute route purists should bear in mind that the 'official' Sustrans route still includes two sections of unsurfaced off-road on the Whinlatter Pass including a bone-janglingly difficult descent that are wholly unmanageable on a road bike and that have not, unlike elsewhere, been given a designated official road-bike suitable alternative. Fortunately, they do have an excellent and straightforward road-bike alternative that is taken by the majority of C2C riders. While the authors of this guide are generally route purists, the rugged descent of Whinlatter on its own hardly justifies leaving the road bike at home. That said, if you love off-road cycling, then some of the other sections might tip the balance. Significantly, the magnificent unsurfaced Waskerley Way from Parkhead Station is entirely viable for road bikes. However, it is prudent to carry a spare inner tube and ensure road bike tyres are at the correct PSI to avoid pinch points. Likewise, 28mm rather than 25mm tyres are advantageous. The Sunderland finish is slightly more taxing for road bikes than Tynemouth, but nonetheless perfectly viable.

Other unsurfaced off-road options require, at the very least, a hybrid bicycle and these give considerable food for thought (see Unsurfaced off-road options in this introduction).

Many people would say that the ideal C2C vehicle is a **gravel bike**, **hybrid** or **tourer** with 32, 35 or 38mm tyres; this would provide more comfort on the above-mentioned sections and allow cyclists the flexibility of adding the great off-road sections over Whinlatter, to Nenthead, from Rookhope and even the challenging Old Coach Road into the itinerary. Likewise, these kinds of bikes are also better for those carrying lots of luggage.

THE COAST TO COAST CYCLE ROUTE

Some people do ride the whole C2C on **mountain bikes**, but this would be frustratingly slow and heavy going as – even if you take all the off-road options – the majority of the route is still on tarmac. If determined to use a mountain bike, it might be worth changing to tyres that will reduce resistance for the road sections.

Tandems are a common sight on the C2C and the main route described is recommended for tandemists. Experienced tandemists should be able to stay in the saddle with perhaps a few exceptions – the climb out of Garrigill being the foremost of these. The willingness of rail operators to accept tandems on trains and the space and provision for them varies. As well as checking with rail operators when planning your journey, the Tandem Club's website gives a good breakdown of what the existing rules are. National Express coaches may accept tandems and can prove an alternative to rail.

The **e-bike** revolution is well and truly underway and these are increasingly common on the C2C, providing opportunity for people who might otherwise be unable to complete the route. Batteries will need recharging at overnight stops. Some e-bikers have found it helpful to give their battery a quick top-up boost at lunch stops in the hilly Pennines. Plugging in will of course be at the discretion of vendors, but the kWh cost should not total more than 10p–30p, even in an age of soaring energy prices.

Tandemists in Garrigill, having tested their mettle on Flinty Fell (Stage 2)

UNSURFACED OFF-ROAD OPTIONS

As of 2022, the C2C is overwhelmingly more commonly tackled by tourers on road bikes. The traffic-free sections in our main route description are all rideable on road bikes, although 28mm tyres are advantageous.

Nonetheless, the C2C was originally intended as a touring route with off-road passages always part of the original or optional route lines. Some of the oft-ignored unsurfaced sections continue to form part of the official primary route line and many riders continue to seek out good off-road passages. The pros and cons of each unsurfaced passage are set out below:

Whinlatter (ascent)

Part of the official primary route. Not passable on a road bike. This option involves steady ups and downs within a shady forest and is pleasant enough on a hybrid or gravel bike. Forestry work can affect access: this section was closed for tree-felling during 2022.

Whinlatter (descent)

Part of the official primary route. Not passable on a road bike. In theory, there is a lot to recommend this shady descent through the forest, particularly when the trees open up to give views of Skiddaw that, although they are also granted on the road option, are even more photogenic here. The descent begins enjoyably enough on wide forest tracks, but soon coalesces into a bone-janglingly tough outing that involves a couple of steep passages of 1 in 4 on loose and rough terrain. Caution is needed and the brakes of any heavily-laden tourers will get a work out. In its favour, the somewhat disconcertingly fast road descent is negated and the return on the back road to Braithwaite is wonderful. Note: in ascent on an east–west ride this is brutal and will almost certainly involve some bike-pushing.

Old Coach Road

Official alternative. Not passable on a road bike. Mountain bikes – which are not really practicable for the C2C – would come into their own on this tough terrain. One fellow female off-road veteran pithily likened the Old Coach Road to childbirth: it's appallingly painful but somehow you find yourself wanting to do it all over again. She was not far off the mark. You'll be cursing the extremely long climb over Threlkeld Knotts, but elated at the unparalleled views of Blencathra and the superb lofty section over Matterdale Common. This is a route rightly beloved of off-road enthusiasts, but the authors' balanced advice would be to save it for a day when you are not trying to get across the country. The Old Coach Road will definitely add a couple of hours onto your cycling and will sap a huge amount of your energy. It is, however, much more viable on an east to west C2C trip. Opting for the Old Coach Road means roughly 16 miles

THE COAST TO COAST CYCLE ROUTE

The Old Coach Road is a serious off-road undertaking (Stage 1)

of alternative C2C ride is used to connect Keswick with Greystoke.

Hartside Top off-road route
Official alternatives. Not passable on a road bike. Two unsurfaced off-road alternatives can be found on the Hartside Top climb. The first, from Five Lane Ends near Renwick, is atrociously uneven, bumpy and loose. It would be challenging enough on a quad bike and has nothing to recommend it. The next alternative comes in two parts and theoretically has value in avoiding any riding on the A road until Hartside Top summit is reached. Unfortunately, the advantage ceases as the long first part is a grassy, peaty and often muddy affair that makes a direct beeline towards the summit of Hartside Top. Its upper part after crossing the A road is a neat if fairly steep gravel track that cuts out a very long hairpin on the A road. Overall, the Hartside alternatives may be fun in descent east–west, if you like that sort of thing; they are little fun in ascent and are best avoided.

Garrigill–Nenthead via Priorsdale
Official alternative. Not passable on a road bike. Topping out at 573m – a negligible 25m lower than the primary route over Flinty Fell – this hardly saves the legs. However, the majority of the route is excellent and recommended for gravel bikes, hybrids and tourers. Unfortunately, the first 400m from Garrigill involves a virtually unrideable steep rubble track, so it may be wise to use the first part of the road route to dodge the rubble – although, that does mean ascending the steepest section of road on the entire C2C! Thereafter, the off-road route climbs on remote and pretty much traffic-free tarmac before descending gradually on a pleasant gravel track to the Nenthead mines complex. Allows a visit to the impressive Ashgill Force.

Nenthead to Black Hill
Official alternative – not recommended. Not passable on a road bike. This short section is surely only for those who enjoy pain. It is not remotely pleasant in ascent or descent. It was beyond either of the

Descending the tricky track from Black Hill to Nenthead (Stage 2)

authors' off-road skill levels to stay in the saddle on a hybrid on this, and one of us even fell off while descending it.

Rookhope to Parkhead Station via Bolts Law Standing Engine
Official off-road option – strongly recommended. Not passable on a road bike. This impressive and memorable passage is unquestionably the best of the unsurfaced off-road options. After an initial steep burst from Rookhope, the climbing becomes gradual. Although it is slow going on a loose aggregate that is at times admittedly fairly challenging, it is not prohibitively so and most will enjoy this ascent before a former moorland railway allows for rapid and delightful progress. Note: this option also has the massive benefit of cutting out the climb over to Stanhope and the troublesome ascent of the ferocious Crawleyside Bank thereafter.

Parkhead Station to Tynemouth/ Sunderland (initially on the Waskerley Way)
Official route. Suitable for road bikes and described in the main route description. Overall, the Sunderland approach is slightly less road-bike friendly than the Tynemouth one.

GETTING THERE AND BACK

By train
For small groups and solo travellers, the train is a viable and environmentally friendly option to get to and

Traffic jam on Coalcleugh Moor with the road down from Black Hill stretching away (Stage 2)

from the start of the route. All UK rail operators carry accompanied bikes free of charge, but different operators on your journey may want you to reserve a space for your bike when you book your ticket. Whitehaven and Workington are connected to the West Coast Mainline at Lancaster and Carlisle by the slow and looping Cumbrian Coast Railway. Tynemouth and Sunderland connect to the East Coast Mainline at Newcastle. To get from Tynemouth to Newcastle mainline station, refer to the Bikes on the Metro section at the end of Day 3. For those leaving a car on the west coast, the Tyne Valley Railway connects Newcastle to Carlisle, where a change of trains is necessary to transfer to the Cumbrian Coast Railway. The fastest time from Newcastle to Whitehaven is 2hr 53min and Newcastle to Workington is just a couple of minutes faster. Be aware – especially if intending to drive home from the west coast – that journeys nearer five hours are not uncommon. No reservations are needed to take bikes on these trains. While these trains do not have to carry more than two bicycles at a time if they are busy, this seems to be down to the discretion of the staff and no problems have been reported. It is possible to leave a car in Whitehaven or Workington and catch trains back from Sunderland or Newcastle.

With vehicles and parking

Driving to the start of the route and returning by train at the end is a fairly popular option. Parking at the beginning and end of the route needs a little thought. At Whitehaven, free parking away from the town centre and cycling back in is possible. Careful consideration of local residents is a priority. The long stay car park on Preston Street CA28 9DL (surveilled) is a convenient option. This is on the opposite side of the road from Haven Cycles and the small retail park. The car park has a daily charge of £6, at the time of going to print. Haven Cycles also offers secure car parking (phone ahead: 01946 63263). There are no restrictions for parking at the Workington route start. The best picking-up point in Tynemouth is the free Priors Haven car park on Pier Road NE30 4DG, but this, like several other free car parks nearby, has a maximum stay of 2 hours no return. There are paid car parks at the top of the Spanish Battery and on Oxford Street. Residential parking is limited and less than ideal. Secure long-term and overnight parking for £7.50 a day is offered by the multi-storey car park at the Beacon Centre North Shields (phoning ahead is recommended: 0191 2583909).

Some groups choose to have a support vehicle – a family member or friend who drives to meet them at the end of each day. Support vehicles are strongly discouraged from driving large sections of the actual route as this is seriously inconsiderate to other cyclists.

With private return transport

This is a popular option for groups of cyclists. A company takes you and your bikes between Tynemouth/ Sunderland and Whitehaven/ Workington either before you start or after you complete the ride. A large number of companies organise a package combining both accommodation and return transport between start and end points. For smaller groups, several companies also offer the option of transporting your vehicle conveniently to the end of the route. Details of companies currently offering these services are in Appendix B.

By bike

It is worth considering combining the C2C with one of two other classic Sustrans coast-to-coast routes: viable options are Hadrian's Cycleway or the Reivers Route. Hadrian's Cycleway begins in Ravenglass, but passes through Whitehaven on its route to South Shields or Tynemouth. The Reivers Route meanwhile begins in Whitehaven and ends at Tynemouth.

WHERE TO STAY

All itineraries for the C2C take account of availability of accommodation. Advanced accommodation booking is recommended, even if camping. Bear in mind that beds in the most popular spots fill up quickly, particularly on summer weekends and in the more remote Pennine section of the route. Generally speaking, if you are prepared to be flexible about where you stay, there is ample accommodation on route for two, three and four day itineraries. Late bookers will always find somewhere to stay in Keswick, Penrith or Alston, when the smaller villages on route are full.

Bed and breakfast accommodation is the most popular option, though bear in mind that not all serve evening meals. This saves on weight and the hassle of buying or making breakfast (although the jury is out on whether fry-ups and big hills first thing in the morning are a good mix!). Other choices such as pubs, hostels, bunkhouses and self-catering are included in the accommodation lists where they are convenient for the route. Over the years, a good selection of group dorm or bunkhouse accommodation has sprung up on route, catering to bigger C2C teams on a budget. Although some places require minimum two night stays, it is worth searching popular self-catering websites such as AirBnb, as some of these can serve C2C cyclists well.

Camping is perfectly possible on route and is the purists' self-sufficient way of enjoying the C2C. It probably goes without saying that the considerable added weight of camping equipment on your bike makes the hills significantly harder.

All accommodation details are listed in Appendix A. If booking accommodation is a hassle, there are a number of companies who offer a transport and accommodation package listed in Appendix B.

BEFORE SETTING OFF ON YOUR BIKE

If, like us, there are limits to your mechanical expertise, then it is well worth taking your bike to the local shop for a pre-C2C service. For the cost – which might only be £20 if everything is in order – weigh up the inconvenience of having to do any major running repairs en route or having to quit the ride. Make sure that your bike is set up correctly – you will be on it for long consecutive stretches.

Tyre pressure

It is wise to check tyre pressures before setting out on any long ride, but with the mixed surfaces of the C2C, particularly so. Tyres usually have a suggested pressure range on their sides. For reference, standard road bike tyres typically suggest a very high pressure of 80–110psi. This can reduce resistance and help avoid pinch points and flats. However, such pressure is difficult to achieve without a track pump and lower pressures can be advantageous, reduce vibration and be counter-intuitively faster. Hybrid tyres often require around 40–50psi.

EQUIPMENT

Ensure you do not forget the following:
- bike lights
- bell
- spare inner tube or tubes (know how to change these before setting off)
- tyre levers

- pump
- Allen keys
- puncture repair kit
- small first aid kit
- a lightweight bike lock may be useful

Hydration and emergency energy food are important on this ride: the hills are challenging. Plan ahead carefully for the section from Langwathby to Nenthead in particular: the loss of the much-loved Hartside Top café, and the unhelpful Saturday afternoon closing and disappointingly limited wares of Garrigill Post Office, can make for a very long stretch without sustenance (although the George and Dragon Inn in Garrigill is due to re-open Easter 2023). Fortunately, there is a mains-water pump to refill bottles in Garrigill.

CARRYING YOUR GEAR

In cycle touring, travelling light is a top priority.

Saddle packs with capacities up to 17 litres are recommended. These are amazingly simple storage for those able to travel light. They avoid the wind resistance of panniers. Other saddle bags, seat packs, triangular frame bags and handlebar bags can

Crawleyside Bank is the last really challenging climb of the route (Stage 3)

also be good options to provide extra accessible storage.

Panniers are a long-standing good choice for cycle tourers. A rack frame is needed in order to use them. Some form of frame can be fitted to most types of bike, although road bikes generally need clamp-style racks. Cyclists carrying lots of camping equipment might add front panniers. If you have never ridden with panniers before, it is advisable to do a few practice rides fully loaded before you set out on a multi-day tour.

Heavy rucksacks put undue strain on necks whilst cycling and should be avoided, but a small daysack could be a viable option for those travelling light.

WHAT TO WEAR

Helmets
We recommend them – they are obviously beneficial in event of an accident or collision, but it comes down to personal preference. There is no current UK law forcing cyclists to wear helmets. In their favour, helmets are now lightweight and allow airflow to the head.

Clothing
Most people will find that cycling-specific clothing is useful. Cycling shorts or tights are padded in the right areas and improve comfort during long days in the saddle. Cycling jerseys usually have several useful features: high-visibility colours, reflective strips, dropped backs to avoid a draughty gap and easily accessible back pockets – it is amazing how much gear and food you can cram into these. Waterproof, windproof and thermal layers are also especially important due to the remote and elevated nature of this ride. Many feel cycling gloves give better grip and reduce handlebar vibration. They are a very good idea outside of summer, as is an earband. Cycling glasses are especially useful if wearing contact lenses or prone to runny eyes.

Footwear
Footwear is a matter of personal choice: most types of trainer will suffice and there is good, if counter-intuitive, university-led research to suggest lightweight trainers have some physiological advantages over specific clip-in cycling shoes. Nonetheless, many cyclists prefer clip-in shoes. Some seasoned cycle-tourers also carry Crocs or flip-flops to change into for evening relaxation. The key tip is to wear tried and tested footwear – a three day tour is not the place to try out new shoes.

MAPS AND APPS

The maps in this book, along with the detailed route descriptions, should provide everything you need to do the C2C. For those who prefer electronic maps, due to the remote nature of the ride, we advise downloading mapping

The Derwent Walk rail path before Rowland's Gill (Stage 3)

in advance and taking this book or – if you can still get one – a paper map as a backup. Unfortunately, the Sustrans Sea to Sea 1:100,000 has been out of print for some time. A 1:90,000 2018 Footprint paper route map is still available to buy online at the time of writing. For those who wish to have more detailed paper mapping, the route is covered at 1:50,000 scale by the following OS Landranger sheets: 89, 90, 91, 87 and 88. The Ordnance Survey now offers access to all its British maps on mobile devices for a reasonable fee – the detail of the OS 1:25,000 mapping can be useful. The app now includes a great National Cycle Network overlay which can be used with GPS devices. This is well worth the investment, especially for those who are also keen walkers. Other apps such as OutdoorActive allow users to access parts of OS mapping for a small fee and use Opencyclemap to provide larger-scale free maps.

SIGNAGE

The C2C is signed with small blue pointer signs of the National Cycle Network, mainly showing the route numbers. As of 2022, there were signs at most significant junctions going west to east and east to west. Signs take the form of blue stickers with white arrows on lampposts and road sign posts or full blue signs bearing white numbers in a red box. The C2C follows the 71 (both Workington and Whitehaven options are designated as 71) to Greystoke, then the 7 to Sunderland or if finishing in Tynemouth changes to the 14 at

Consett to the Tyne, the 141 to cross the Tyne, and the 72 to the sea. The 14 continues as the Keelman's Way (not recommended).

USING THIS GUIDE

The C2C is described in detail in three day stage chapters. Each has a summary of what to expect on the day ahead, along with a comprehensive route description and detailed maps, at a smaller scale where the route goes through populated areas. Points at which it is important to pay attention to the navigation are highlighted, as well as potential hazards. Also included in each day section is a route profile, showing where the main climbs and descents of the day take place.

Route information boxes for each chapter provide key information you need to know before going on the ride such as mileage, ascent and refreshment stops. Total approximate ascents are from OS data and the gradients refer to the steepest parts of the climbs. Details of worthwhile variations are given at the appropriate points within the route description.

Details of distances, ascents, stops and refreshments are given, but cyclists should refer to the main text for a detailed description of the route.

GPX tracks

GPX tracks for the routes in this guidebook are available to download free at www.cicerone.co.uk/1118/GPX. If you have not bought the book through the Cicerone website, or have bought the book without opening an account, please register your purchase in your Cicerone library to access GPX and update information.

A GPS device is an excellent aid to navigation, but you should also carry a map and compass and know how to use them. GPX files are provided in good faith, but in view of the profusion of formats and devices, neither the author nor the publisher accepts responsibility for their use. We provide files in a single standard GPX format that works on most devices and systems, but you may need to convert files to your preferred format using a GPX converter such as gpsvisualizer.com or one of the many other apps and online converters available.

Looking into West Allendale, above Nenthead, from beyond Coalcleugh (Stage 2)

THE C2C

The Coast to Coast Cycle Route

DAY 1
Whitehaven to Greystoke

Start	Whitehaven (NX 969 182)
Finish	Greystoke (NY 440 309)
Distance	47 miles (76km)
Total ascent	1251m
Steepest climb	Whinlatter Pass – one of the great Lakeland hill climbs (peaks at 1 in 4 main route, or 1 in 5 recommended route)
Terrain	Surfaced cycle paths, otherwise minor roads predominate. At Whinlatter, there are unsurfaced-track or road options.
OS maps	Landranger 89 and 90 Route signed as 71 or C2C.
Refreshments	Kirkstile Inn, Loweswater (just off route), Lorton (excellent café/shop and pub), Braithwaite (café, pub and shop), Keswick, Threlkeld (excellent café and pub), Scales (pub), Mungrisdale (pub).
Intermediate distances	Rowrah, 9 miles; Loweswater, 16 miles; Lorton, 21 miles; Braithwaite, 26 miles; Keswick, 30 miles, Threlkeld, 34 miles and Mungrisdale 38 miles.

The first leg of the C2C is a great day's riding in anyone's book. From Whitehaven cyclists are eased into action on 9 miles of former railway with a virtually imperceptible upwards incline. This allows for a rapid transition from coast to Lake District. The first two miles are a slightly scrappy affair and the route is slow to reveal its hand. When it does, swathes of Lakeland scenery become the delectable flavour of the rest of the day. Intermittent climbing gains the lapping shores of Loweswater, with Ennerdale Water, Crummock Water, Bassenthwaite Lake and Derwentwater also part of the tour. On fair days, high fells make up the skyline: Pillar, Grasmoor, Skiddaw and most impressively of all, Blencathra vie for attention. After a peaceful journey through the Vale of Lorton, Whinlatter Pass, the day's test piece climb, rears its head and presents pristine forest scenery. The honeypot of Keswick is escaped by the bridges and tunnels of the excellent revamped rail path in the Greta

Day 1 – Whitehaven to Greystoke

valley that leads to the pleasant, Threlkeld. Thereafter, a superb and little-known minor road leads to Mungrisdale. Taking the recommended route, the gradual climb over Berrier Hill to the attractive village of Greystoke adds Hellvellyn and High Street to the day's smorgasbord of panoramic Lakeland delights.

The route sets out from the **Marina** in Whitehaven. This has seen good investment over the last thirty years and is a pleasant place for a 'grand depart'. There is a large C2C sculpture by the water's edge on the first slipway on the south side of the marina. This denotes the official starting point and is a suitable place to dip a wheel in the Irish Sea.

Dipping the traditional wheel at the route's Whitehaven start

THE COAST TO COAST CYCLE ROUTE

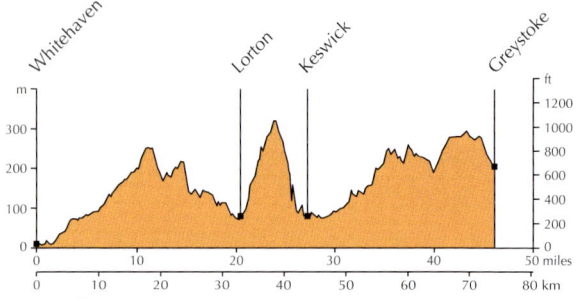

The official start point is easily reached from Whitehaven rail station. Cycle out of the car park past a superstore and turn right on the main road into town. Take the first left (signed NCN route 10), then cut left almost immediately onto the seafront path, where the sculpture is easily located.

Whitehaven's distinctive Candlestick chimney vented a mineshaft of the former **Wellington Pit**, the scene of Cumbria's worst mining disaster in 1910 when 132 miners lost their lives. There are two monuments to the tragedy here, along with a recently commissioned mosaic.

Whitehaven has a rich **sea-faring history**, which is recognised by its maritime museum and an annual festival. In 1778 the town was attacked by the proto U.S. Navy commanded by John Paul Jones during the American War of Independence.

From the C2C sculpture on the marina slipway turn right (towards the Candlestick chimney) to the nearby T-junction with Quay Street. Turn left on this, then right at the next T-junction and follow the sometimes busy road away from the coast for 400m until, just after passing over a mini roundabout by a retail park, a poorly accessed sharp left turn allows escape onto a cycle path.

A road is soon crossed requiring a brief right, then immediate left to join a drive passing Whitehaven's rugby

Day 1 – Whitehaven to Greystoke

and football grounds. This leads to a cycle path that soon swings left to pass under the railway line via a disconcertingly low tunnel. It is followed by a snaking weave up to an estate road. Turn right and after 200m trend right again to join another section of cycle path. This passes back under the railway line before emerging onto another estate lane. Head straight on for 100m then turn left before the bend and cross a little green to join another

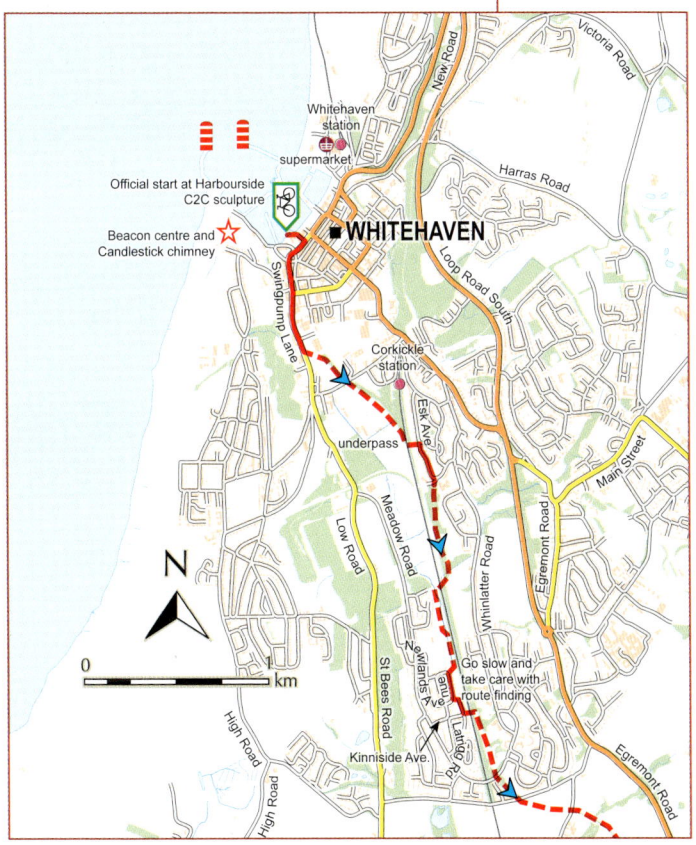

street. After 60m on this, a sharp left under the rail line is taken. At the triangular green trend right and shortly afterwards bear slightly left following commemorative blue metal mining posts that sign Cleator Moor, Frizington, Rowrah and Kirkland. You are now on a well-signed uninterrupted 7½ mile section of cycle path (only marred by tree roots) that evokes a sense of freedom and soon brings the north-eastern Lakeland fells into view.

At **Rowrah**, the surfaced rail path comes to an end and a ramp leads up to join an unsurfaced track. This narrows into a short-lived unsurfaced path through High Leys Nature Reserve. Exit onto the road and turn left. At the crossroads head right past Kirkland Primary School to climb over the brow of the hill – the impressive valley to the right is Ennerdale, with Pillar (892m), Steeple (819m) Little Scoat Fell (841m) and, at the head of the dale, the glorious north face of Great Gable (899m).

Head straight down at the crossroads and commence a delightful climb over the photogenic shoulder

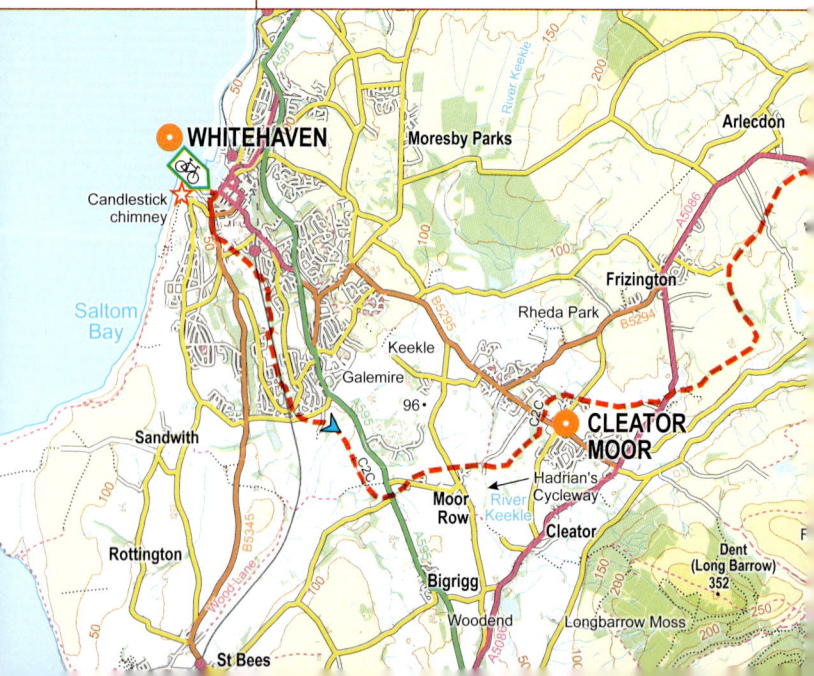

THE COAST TO COAST CYCLE ROUTE

Looking across at Bowness Knott and the Ennerdale fells

of Keltonfell. Turn left at the T-junction to eventually descend pleasantly towards Lamplugh. At the T-junction, turn right and climb through **Lamplugh** passing the red sandstone St Michael's church before taking a right turn signed to Loweswater. At the farm the road bends eastwards to begin a steep descent of the brilliantly named Fangs Brow towards Loweswater. ◄

The imposing mountain looming over the south-eastern end of Loweswater is Mellbreak – one of the great stand-alone Lakeland fells. The hotel at the foot of Fangs Brow sometimes has an honesty box for flapjacks and cakes.

> Lesser-known **Loweswater** is the northernmost link in a lovely chain that includes Buttermere – which it was once joined to – and Crummock Water. It is a tempting place to take a dip, but watch out for the periodic blue-green algae blooms, which have blighted the lake in recent years.

Continue on the narrow road past **Loweswater**. Limited climbing soon brings Crummock Water and the impressive Grasmoor (852m) into view. A left turn is now taken – signed Thackthwaite. ◄ Continue pleasantly on the undulating back road through Thackthwaite towards Lorton. At the T-junction turn right (the Workington start

The nearby Kirkstile Inn is 200m past the turning and reached by the next right.

Day 1 – Whitehaven to Greystoke

joins here) and cross a bridge over the River Cocker to reach **Low Lorton**.

The wonderful sprawling historic village of **Lorton** (strictly speaking Low Lorton and High Lorton) – is a good place to stop and has a pub 200m off route and an excellent wooden village shop/café oft-frequented by C2C riders – seating/bike parking down the narrow side path.

The unfortunate Mary Robinson, popularly known as the **'Maid of Buttermere'** was married to the unscrupulous bigamist John Hatfield or as she thought 'Colonel Hope' in Lorton's impressive 12th century church in 1802. The gargantuan **Lorton Yew** or 'Wordsworth's Yew Tree' witnessed it all and can be visited at the Scales turning at Boonbeck – incidentally behind the site of the original Jennings Brewery. The tree, with its 8m girth, is more than 1,000 years old and has withstood the ravages of the many storms which have wreaked havoc on this area. It is immortalised by Lakeland poet William Wordsworth in his poem Yew Trees:

Skirting Loweswater in a peaceful corner of Lakeland

'Of vast circumference and gloom profound | This solitary Tree! -a living thing | Produced too slowly ever to decay; | Of form and aspect too magnificent | To be destroyed'.

At the offset crossroads the route heads straight on. At the bend just after the village shop/café two options for overcoming the great Lakeland climb to Whinlatter Pass present themselves.

The present official route – originally intended as a temporary diversion – continues around the bend for 20m to a right turn up a road signed 'Unsuitable for Motor Vehicles'. This narrow hill ratchets up to a short-lived but feisty 1 in 4 before relenting to filter onto the main B road. Turn right, initially passing through a delightful tunnel of beech trees and continue climbing towards the pass, which comes in stages and allows for recovery. The second-trickiest part of the ascent quickly announces itself by means of the Scawgill Bridge near Spout Force. Here, a shady but steep 1 in 6 weaves up through the trees; ensure the steeper inside line is taken on the blind bend (the gradient soon eases). In 500m, the original route – now a recommended alternative – via Scales Farm joins from the right.

Original route

The original and better route is to turn right signed to Scales, cross over the delightful Boon Beck by Wordsworth's yew tree and follow the road which soon steepens to peak at 1 in 5. The cycling then eases into a less severe gradient. Although slightly harder than the main B road, this is a truly wonderful climb on an almost always car-free road which allows for a steady and consistent rhythm to develop. This is joined from the right by another road coming up from Hopebeck. A short descent adds great variety to the journey up Whinlatter, before a brief climb joins the B road.

Roughly 800m further up the pass after the Scales Farm/Hopebeck road joins the B Road, the official C2C signs the first of two passages of unsurfaced riding on

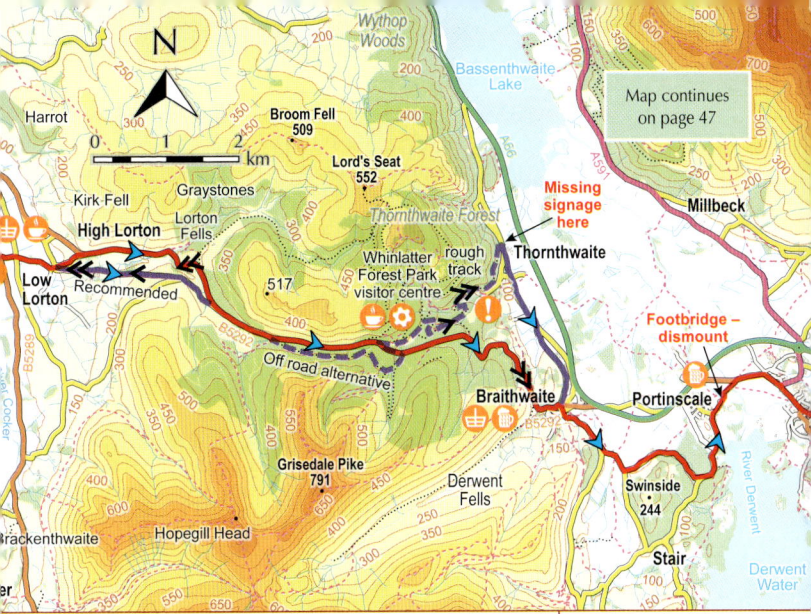

Whinlatter. Notably, these are the only parts of the official C2C route not given an official road bike-suitable alternative (although the majority of riders opt for the straightforward road descent, regardless). Cyclists have two options.

Road-bike option

Those on road bikes should categorically eschew the official route at this point and avoid the forest trails to stay on the B road to the top of the Whinlatter Pass (café, osprey-watch camera, information, bike hire, tourist shop). Thereafter, continue down the road taking considerable care on the extremely fast descent to Braithwaite, which gives sensational views of the Skiddaw Massif midway. On entering **Braithwaite**, follow the main road leftwards along a narrowing between houses and a steep hillside, then immediately after the sharp bend rightwards take an unsigned right turn onto a minor road before the Royal Oak pub. (The off-road descent of Whinlatter rejoins the road option here.)

Official off-road route (not suitable for road bikes)
Whinlatter's two off-road passages use only broad forest tracks – if you find yourself on anything narrow, you have gone wrong. Follow the blue 71 signage, ignoring the many mountain biking and hiking trails that Whinlatter is now famous for. The 71 signage directs riders on a gradual off-road climb over the pass. After a mile, a T-junction is reached where a left leads down beside a car park back to the B road. Here, another left doubles back up to the apex of the road pass.

A right is now taken into the Whinlatter Pass complex – stay on the initially surfaced main track between the visitor centre and the car parks. At the first track fork just beyond the Cyclewise shop, head straight on ignoring the left track uphill. At the next fork, bear right downhill. After 100m, a sharp right turn/bend is taken at a T-junction of forest tracks. This route snakes its way round the hillside. Stay left at the next fork. Soon after this, at a bend, a 1 in 4 descent proves bone-janglingly tricky and requires considerable care if heavily loaded. The way is now straightforward if steep and bumpy occasionally. Emerging from the forest onto a minor road, turn right and then right again onto the B road towards Braithwaite. After a mile, take a right turn up a lovely minor road that climbs over a shoulder of Braithwaite How before descending into **Braithwaite** proper. Go straight across the road at The Royal Oak pub (the road descent of Whinlatter joins here).

> **Whinlatter Forest** bills itself as England's only true mountain forest. In recent years, it has become a mountain biking mecca, with adventurous trails to suit both novices and experts. The visitor centre (café and bike shop) has a live video feed of the osprey nest at Bassenthwaite and red squirrels are common nearby. Descending from the pass, riders will see Derwent Water and to the north, Bassenthwaite Lake. Bassenthwaite is the only 'lake' in the Lake District: all the other watery masses are named Water, Mere or Tarn. Close to

Day 1 – Whitehaven to Greystoke

where the off-road route descends to Thornthwaite from Whinlatter, two white beacons can be seen on the hillside of Barf. These were reputably placed there to mark the demise of the hapless Bishop of Derry and his clerk, who perished during a drunken horseback race up the hillside.

Main route

A minor road leads out of Braithwaite (pub, shop, café) serving up further sumptuous views of Skiddaw. After 1 mile, a left turn signed to Ullock is taken. At the T-junction, filter left downhill and head onwards to the centre of **Portinscale** where a right turn off the bend is taken to access a footbridge over the River Derwent (cyclists dismount). At the T-junction turn right on the main road into Keswick, continue straight on at the mini roundabout. The road bends sharply leftwards then rightwards to negotiate the pedestrianised centre of **Keswick**. Soon after, at the brow of a short gradual rise, a sharp left is taken downhill crossing the easily missed River Greta and passing by Keswick Youth Hostel and Fitz Park. Come off left at the first bend and cycle up to the leisure centre on a shared-use path. This is followed rightwards round

Skiddaw looms over the footbridge at Portinscale

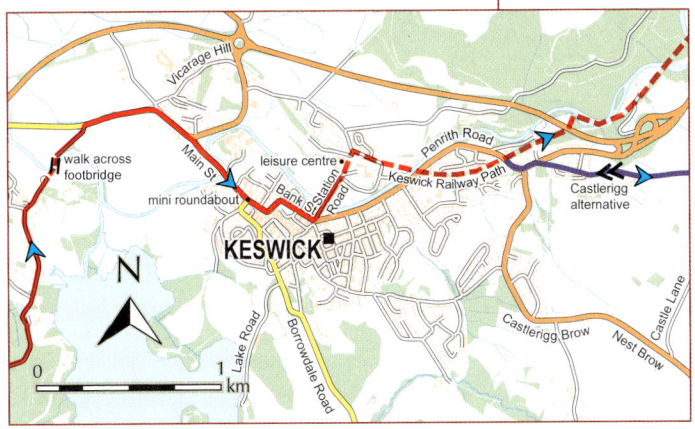

the leisure centre to where a right turn now leads to the former Keswick railway station.

The bustling town of **Keswick** needs no introduction. It is justifiably popular with holidaymakers and has plenty – including a pencil museum! – to distract cyclists who are planning to make an overnight stop. Its name comes from Kese-wik meaning cheese farm. The town is sheltered by the mass of the Skiddaw group, some of the oldest mountains in the Lake District.

THE KESWICK–THRELKELD RAILWAY PATH

The Keswick–Threlkeld railway path is a superbly engineered section of traffic-free riding, linking the bustling heart of the northern Lakes with the quiet village of Threlkeld, which nestles under the precipitous slopes of Blencathra. In 2015, Storm Desmond and its accompanying floods decimated the route – two of the crucial bridges spanning the River Greta were washed away and three more seriously damaged. After a mammoth rebuilding programme, the much-loved route finally reopened in 2020. A highlight is the new Bobbin Mill tunnel, which clings to the gorgeside at Briery. The Lake District was the bobbin capital of the world in the mid-19th century. **Briery bobbin mill** made bobbins for the silks used in Queen Elizabeth II's wedding dress. The **River Greta**, at 11km long, is one of the shortest rivers in the UK. It boasts diverse wildlife such as otters, trout, salmon, eels, wrens and dippers. **Threlkeld** has a quarry museum along with a geography field centre on the site of a former TB sanatorium. More useful to C2C cyclists, the village has a café and two pubs.

If interested in tackling either of two official alternatives that visit the Castlerigg stone circle, with the second option also tackling the Old Coach Road, see the end of this chapter.

The vast majority of cyclists follow the 3-mile-long railway path straightforwardly to Threlkeld. ◀ The end of the rail path involves a short speed-restricting snake to reach a cycle path beside the busy A66. After 200m on this, a minor road fortunately leads leftwards into the heart of **Threlkeld** (very good café, with public toilets, accessed from rear). Continue through the village until a left onto a dead-end road is taken on a bend. A brief climb brings the south face of Blencathra into sharp focus.

Blencathra from near Wanthwaite on the alternative route

> **Blencathra** is the legendary resting place of King Arthur and his knights. They are said to be lying dormant inside the mountain, but will rise again should the summit ever come under attack.

A pleasant closed road is soon joined by means of a gate. Unfortunately, this concludes before Scales is reached and riders find themselves once more on a segregated cycle path beside the busy A66. This 1km passage detracts from the route. Mercifully an escape is soon made leftwards into **Scales** (pub). A left just after the pub accesses the tremendous back road to Mungrisdale – a truly impressive section of riding, albeit with six – yes six – gates to negotiate. At **Mungrisdale** (pub) a T-junction is reached and two options are possible.

Official option

The official route is unsatisfactory and has never made sense, either psychologically or practicably. The authors strongly recommend ignoring it in favour of the official alternative below (both options have similar levels of ascent). If determined to take this option, turn right and follow the road downhill back to the A66. A left begins a short but somehow simply horrible section of – albeit cycle segregated – cycle path uphill beside the noisy A66. Fortunately, a left turn onto a parallel minor road gives respite. The A66 is joined by more segregated cycle path for a further 200m before a left turn finally leaves the main road behind. Take the first left towards Berrier but after 1km take the first right directly to **Greystoke**, 3 miles away.

> **Greystoke** is famed for being the birthplace of Tarzan, King of the Apes. The character is the son of Lord and Lady Greystoke, who resided at the castle in the village. In Edgar Rice Burroughs' story, the baby boy Tarzan is orphaned and fends for himself in the African jungle, wrestling a few crocodiles and lions along the way. It should be easier going for cyclists at the village, where there is a small shop and pub, although the cycle café is now closed.

Day 1 – Whitehaven to Greystoke

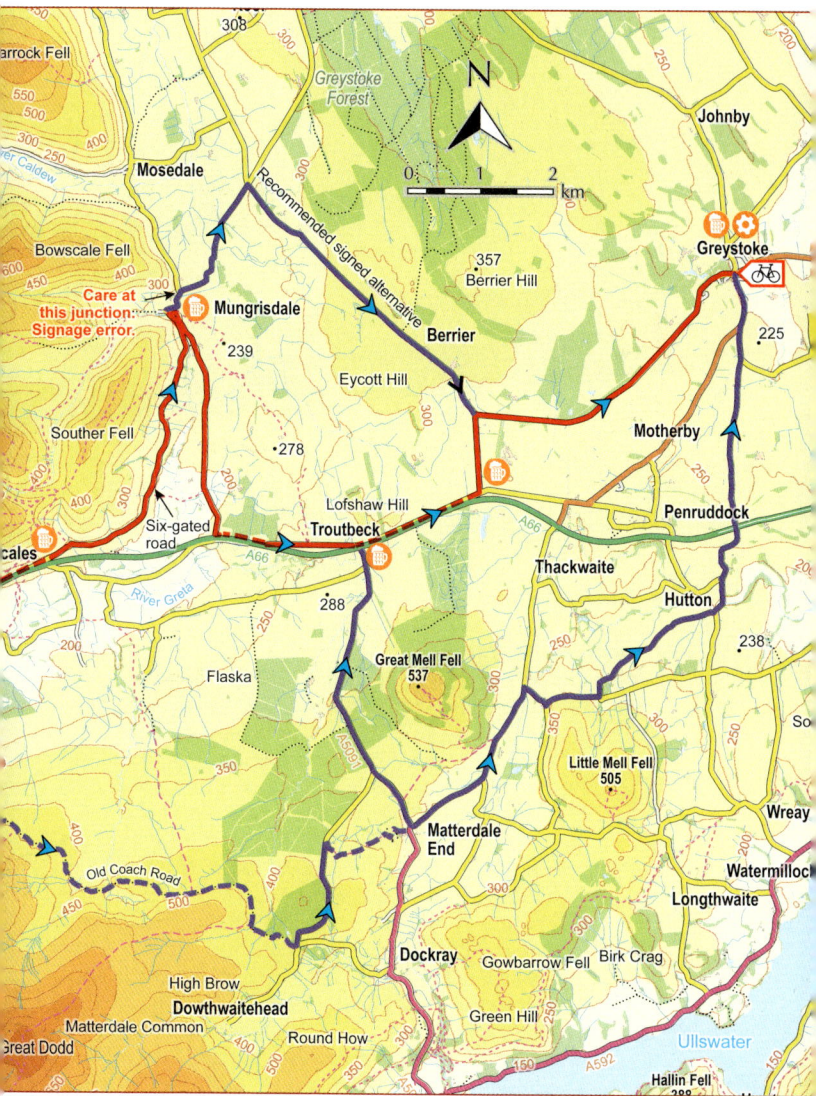

THE COAST TO COAST CYCLE ROUTE

Greystoke: birthplace of Tarzan, Lord of the Apes

Preferred option
A better option is to turn left uphill in **Mungrisdale** and follow the road round through the village. Note: as of 2022, Sustrans have made a mistake with the signage, while the signed Reivers connection route does head straight on, the C2C alternative goes right. Ensure you ignore the C2C sign and turn right signed 'Hutton Roof'. This lovely minor road leads to a crossroads. Turn right and climb steadily over the shoulder of Berrier Hill, soaking up a fine panorama of Lakeland fells that – on clear days – span from High Street (828m), the Helvellyn massif (950m), the Scafell group (978m) and over to the nearby east face of Blencathra (868m) (although its alternative name 'Saddleback' makes sense from this perspective). A fast descent is soon made through the hamlet of **Berrier**, before a left turn leads directly and quickly to **Greystoke** 3 miles away.

Day 1 – Whitehaven to Greystoke

Castlerigg stone circle option (road-bike suitable)
This served as the main route for several years while the Keswick–Threlkeld railway path was being repaired after 2015's Storm Desmond battered the Lakes. From the old Keswick railway station, follow the cycle path over the obvious River Greta. After a further 450m, and just before entering the first tunnel, exit rightwards up a narrow track to meet a gate. **Castlerigg stone circle** is well-served by blue signage from here. Turn right on the main road uphill, then take the first left, followed by a further right soon after. The road now climbs steeply up to the brow of the hill where the stone circle is hidden in a field to the right – use the footpath to access it.

> The incredible setting is the star at the **Castlerigg stone circle**. The monument dates from the Neolithic period around 3,000BC. No-one knows why it was built and legend has it that it is impossible to count the stones – you will always get a different number.

Thereafter, continue straight down the hill and turn right at the next two T-junctions. After 300m a right can be taken to access the very challenging Old Coach Road unsurfaced off-road route (see below). To return to the main route at Threlkeld, head straight on, ensuring you filter onto the cycle path on the right to make use of a traffic island in order to cross the dangerous A66 safely. A segregated cycle path now leads leftwards to join a minor road into **Threlkeld**.

Old Coach Road option (not suitable for road bikes)
It is worth noting that the extremely challenging Old Coach Road option (see Unsurfaced off-road options in the introduction) adopts a very different line all the way to Greystoke, missing out both Threlkeld and Mungrisdale. On the plus side, it avoids any riding beside the A66. Follow the Castlerigg option to the Old Coach Road turning described above. Turn right onto a minor road to reach a T-junction. Turn right here. ▶ After 60m turn left onto a track to begin the Old Coach Road.

> The left C2C turn is a further option to return riders to the main route at Threlkeld and uses the National Route 6; if heading that way, go straight across the A66 and up the gated road.

Approaching Matterdale End on the Old Coach Road alternative

The panoramic vistas of Blencathra begin to give way to the sylvan forests of Matterdale and the Ullswater fells.

Heading through the gate, the 'fun' begins immediately with a challenging steep shady climb that winds through the woods before unveiling inspiring views of Blencathra. This appears to be just about the right side of too steep initially, but it continues more and more painfully until all but the Herculean – and perhaps e-mountain-bikers – will give up trying to ride it. There is scope to go wrong after 1km where the track splits and there is currently no signage. The left-hand way contouring around the hillside is vastly appealing, but unfortunately the route goes straight ahead and straight up the rocky track. After what might seem like many hours of effort, the track reaches a gate onto Matterdale Common. This more comfortable section might finally be the place where you will take stock of the majestic surroundings.

The track still has a few lesser sections of climbing, but is rideable for mere mortals from this point. ◀ Just before reaching a forest, cross an entertaining cobbled ford and then descend slightly to reach a parking area. Turn left on the road for about a mile of blissfully easy riding, then turn sharply back right on a signed track. This descends simply to the reach the hamlet of **Matterdale End**. At the A road in Matterdale End there are two options:

Day 1 – Whitehaven to Greystoke

- Best is to follow the A road leftwards for only 30m and then turn right for 2km on a minor road until a right turn. This climbs fairly steeply but pleasantly before swinging round towards **Thackwaite**, which is reached with a left turn downhill. After one mile bear left at the T-junction – effectively straight on. Climb fairly steeply with superb views south from the top of the hill to reach the A66. Making use of the traffic island, cross directly over the A66 with care and head straight on, turning right on the B road to reach **Greystoke**.
- Alternatively, head left on the A road for 2½ miles to Troutbeck. At the A66 beyond, use the shared-use path on the right to reach a traffic island crossing in 60m. Transfer onto the C2C and head right to join the route into Greystoke.

EAST TO WEST

This day is just as satisfying, if not as equally testing, going from the east. Signage is generally very good – apart from where highlighted below. It is important not to be confused by the Old Coach Road 71 option in **Greystoke** and head uphill out of the village. Likewise, if using the recommended road alternative via **Berrier**, ensure that the left just before Mungrisdale is taken into the village and the misleading sign for the C2C pointing rightwards is ignored. A right at the back of the pub in **Mungrisdale** leads onto the wonderful many-gated back road to **Threlkeld**. The fourth of its six gates comes suddenly after a sharp bend with a steep descent – care needed. The Whinlatter climb via the road-option from **Braithwaite** is hard and sustained on leaving the village, but soon eases and settles into a glorious big climb; it offers periods of shade and shelter, though has some blind bends – ensure single file cycling throughout. The off-road option up Whinlatter has a missing badge after the well-signed left onto the narrow minor road just after **Thornwaite**. Cyclists should take the almost immediate first track left uphill from the narrow minor road. Unless you are Tom Pidcock, expect to do some bike-pushing in parts of this tough off-road ascent, which peaks at 1 in 4 – the challenge has been set! If intending to finish in **Workington**, after crossing the River Cocker in Low Lorton ignore the 71 pointing left and continue round – initially signed Rogerscale. C2C signage for Workington soon materialises.

THE COAST TO COAST CYCLE ROUTE

DAY 1A
Workington to Greystoke

Start	Workington (NX 982 297)
Finish	Greystoke (NY 440 309)
Distance	44 miles (71km)
Total ascent	1191m
Steepest climb	Whinlatter Pass – one of the great Lakeland hill climbs (peaks at 1 in 4 main route, or 1 in 5 recommended route)
Terrain	Surfaced cycle paths, otherwise minor roads predominate. At Whinlatter, there are unsurfaced-track or road options.
OS maps	Landranger 89 and 90 Route signed as 71 or C2C.
Refreshments	Great Broughton, Cockermouth then see Day 1.
Intermediate distances	Cockermouth, 12 miles; Lorton, 18 miles; Braithwaite, 23 miles; Keswick, 27 miles; Threlkeld, 31 miles; Mungrisdale, 35 miles.

Given an image of the square municipal-looking South Pier lighthouse, cyclists might be forgiven for assuming that the Workington starting point is less than ideal. It tends to come as a pleasant surprise to find that both its position and vantage are magnificent. Situated in a quiet out-of-the-way area a mile or so from the urban expanse of Workington, this proves to be a great place to gather thoughts and do last-minute checks before setting out. Indeed, many will greatly prefer this launch pad to the rival one at Whitehaven Marina. The lighthouse has a viewing platform from which to scan across the Irish Sea towards the impressive Galloway Hills that peak with Merrick (843m). Beside the lighthouse is an excellent beach for dipping into the Irish Sea and a convenient no-restrictions car park.

From the lighthouse, the route hardly seems to brush Workington, where it begins to share its course with the Reivers Route and, briefly, Hadrian's Cycleway – two of Sustrans' other coast-to-coast rides. Heading inland, Hadrian's Cycleway branches off and the C2C weaves along surfaced railway paths and quiet minor roads through Great Broughton and Papcastle

Day 1A – Workington to Greystoke

to reach the unspoilt town of Cockermouth – birthplace of William and Dorothy Wordsworth. Here the C2C parts company with the Reivers Route to adopt a slightly indirect but nonetheless interesting and highly enjoyable course that leads to the delightful village of Lorton, where it unites with the Whitehaven option.

Originally the Workington start used an off-road route through Wythop Woods above the A66 near Bassenthwaite Lake. This cut out Lorton and the Whinlatter Pass altogether in favour of joining the Whitehaven route near Braithwaite. All signage for this original route has now been removed and there are no plans to reinstate it. By incorporating Lorton and Whinlatter, the present Workington route is considerably better than its original incarnation.

The proud town of Workington is the home of '**Uppies and Downies**', an idiosyncratic sport played only in Workington: the 'Uppies' are participants traditionally resident in the slightly more affluent upper area of Workington while the 'Downies' are those who – historically at least – would have been resident in the reclaimed marshes, dockland and coastal dwellings. Matches have been recorded as far back as the sixteenth century and are still played annually. They involve upwards of 1,000 players trying to move a ball – usually by means of a scrum – to the opposition's 'goal' across town; this often takes hours.

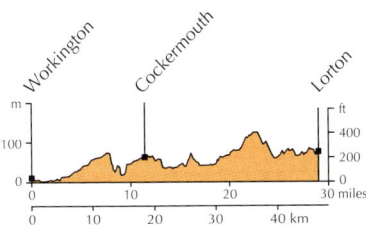

The start of the journey from Workington lighthouse

From the lighthouse, follow the shared-use cycle path straightforwardly inland keeping the road to the right. At a distinctive red and white metal tower, the path turns sharply left utilising the narrow England Coastal Path to pass the sailing club harbour. Here, before it was destroyed by the 2009 floods, the route formerly deployed the Dock Rail and Pedestrian Bridge to cross the Derwent. The amended route is actually better.

The ride now follows Town Quay parallel with a separate inlet of the Derwent. Care is needed with the pronounced speed bumps. At the T junction, turn left onto a bridge to cross over the railway line and then immediately go left again to swing down towards a prominent church mounted above trees. Branch off on the first – easily missed – right below the church and follow the road round the back of the Travelodge. After swinging left downhill a right turn is taken along Griffin Street and through a large car park towards Workington Leisure Centre. Stay to the right of the leisure centre to reach a

DAY 1A – WORKINGTON TO GREYSTOKE

no entry sign that does not apply to cycles. Turn left here to cross the new **Navvies Bridge** (Workington's central shopping area is just through the tunnel on the right).

Continue beyond Navvies Bridge for a further 700m to a junction of paths. Here, Hadrian's Cycleway forks off left, but the C2C goes straight on (as does the Reivers Route). Follow the pleasant former rail line through the **Siddick Ponds Nature Reserve** and **Seaton**. Beyond Seaton, stunning Lakeland views to the right of the path will catch the eye. A rightwards ramp just before a tunnel is taken to leave the rail line and emerge at a minor road above Camerton. The Lakeland fells, most noticeably the Skiddaw massif, become more prominent at this point. ▶

The Siddick Ponds Reserve is one of the best places in Cumbria to spot otters.

Turn right descending steeply through the village of **Camerton**, being careful not to miss a sharp left turn midway down the hill. Take this minor road, which soon presents a brief aperitif of the hills to come. The road joins the edge of the River Derwent, before a middle section

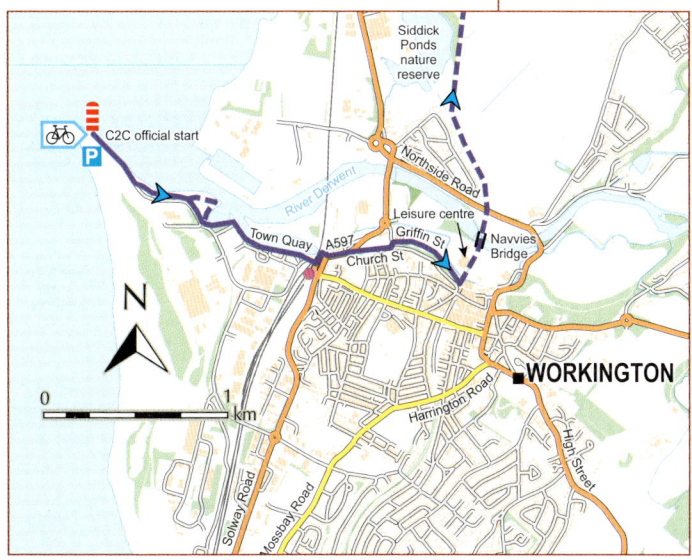

that is closed to motor vehicles. There is a very stiff little climb as the Derwent is left behind. Although straightforward, the signage becomes disconcertingly sparse until **Great Broughton** is reached (pubs, café, shop). Bear right onto the main street towards Cockermouth and continue straight through Great Broughton and, in 200m, take a left – effectively straight on – towards Papcastle.

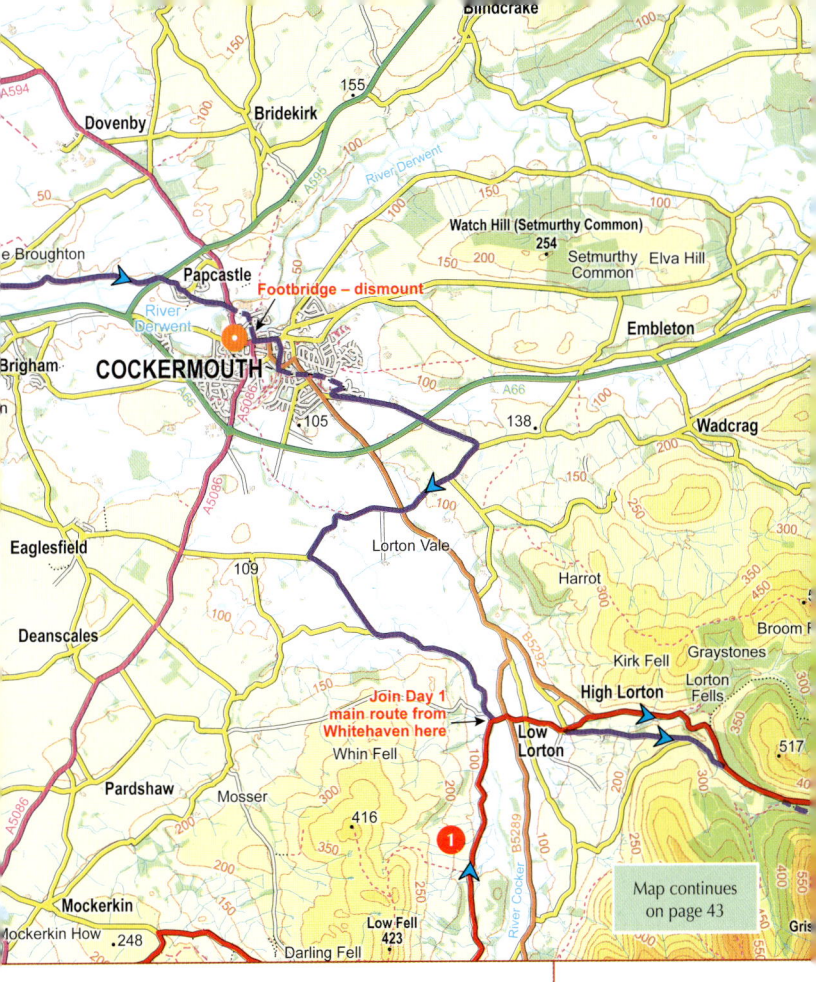

Remains of a substantial **Roman fort** were discovered at Papcastle near the sharp bend in the River Derwent.

Continue on the winding narrow road through **Papcastle** to the A5086. Look for a path opposite (just to the right of the factory gates). Cross the A5086 with

On the cycle path near Camerton with Hopegill Head (left), Grasmoor, Mellbreak (centre), Pillar and Steeple (right)

care and take the path, bearing right when it ends then almost immediately taking a similar path down the side of a car park and over a footbridge to enter **Cockermouth** and reach Main Street, with its independent shops and eateries. Turn left up Main Street to cross an easily missed bridge over the River Cocker, which gives the town its name.

COCKERMOUTH

Cockermouth, home of Jennings Ale, lies just outside the Lake District National Park boundary. Poets William and Dorothy Wordsworth spent their early years here. While Cockermouth does not become overwhelmed by summer tourist hoards, the National Trust-owned Georgian Wordsworth House on Main Street attracts plenty of visitors. Cockermouth was badly hit by floods in 2009; one interesting consequence of the devastation which followed was the discovery of the remains of a large Roman civilian settlement in the vicinity, associated with the nearby Roman fort of Derventio. Fletcher Christian, the most famous mutineer on The Bounty, called Cockermouth home, as did cricketer Ben Stokes, who learnt his trade at the local club.

Day 1A – Workington to Greystoke

> Care is needed with route finding when leaving Cockermouth. The crucial C2C signage on Market Place has been unhelpfully and confusingly pushed round the pole. The shared-use cycle signage that supports access to Cockermouth School may also confuse, as might Cockermouth itself, which can be a little disorientating, especially as the route has been slightly adjusted over the years.

Immediately after the bridge, the Reivers Route (10) branches off left uphill. The C2C turns right onto Market Place, but after only 30m turns right again opposite the Allerdale Court Hotel onto Market Street (the signage

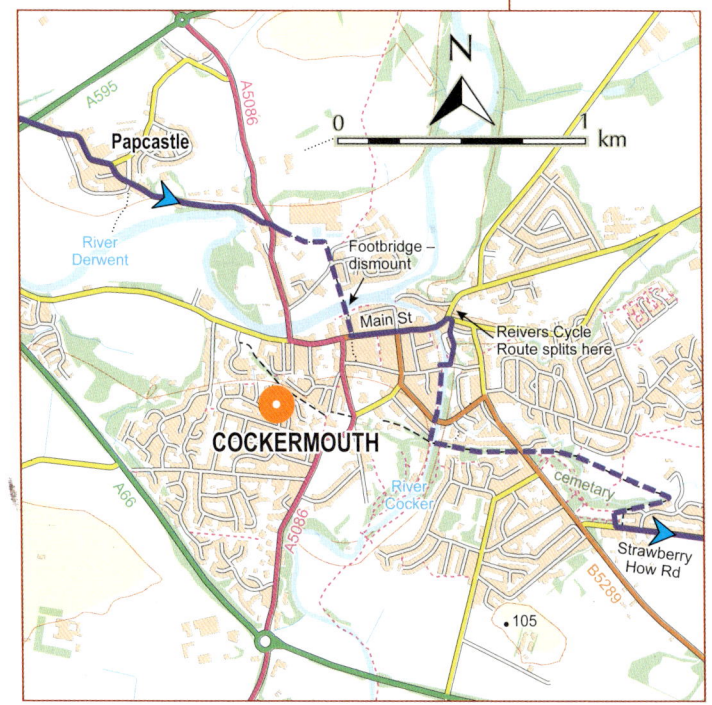

THE COAST TO COAST CYCLE ROUTE

has been mangled here). Head through a first car park to join the river and pass through an arch. At the end of a second car park, take a right over the footbridge. Immediately turn left following the riverside path under a road bridge. Pass under a second bridge belonging to the former Cockermouth railway line, which is accessed by a narrow right uphill.

Follow the cycle path across the old railway bridge to reach a now outdated metal C2C Sunderland/Workington mile marker after 1km. Turn right just before this onto an unlikely unsurfaced narrow path, taking care with loose material. This bumpy path is thankfully short-lived and swings past a cemetery to reach Strawberry How Road. Turn left and continue gradually uphill to a T-junction. Turn right to reach a crossroads. Ignore the B road to Lorton and instead head straight across to swing down and round over the Cocker once more. After a further 600m, take the first left. This leads to Low Lorton and is joined by the Whitehaven start just before the River Cocker is crossed to enter the delightful village. From here follow Day 1 to Greystoke.

Crossing the River Derwent in Cockermouth

DAY 2
Greystoke to Allenheads

Start	Greystoke (NY 404 309)
Finish	Allenheads (NY860 453)
Distance	40 miles (64km)
Total ascent	1533m
Steepest climb	The mammoth Hartside Top is the most daunting, although the ascent from Garrigill presents a ferocious 1 in 4 – gold star if you manage it without a bike push!
Terrain	Primary route entirely on minor roads or, alternative unsurfaced off-road options.
OS maps	Landrangers 91, 92, 87
Refreshments	Newton Reigny (pub); Penrith (all services – though the route does not directly pass cafes etc.); Langwathby (good shop on village green which sells hot drinks, pies etc. open 7 days, pub); Hartside Top (applications have been made to rebuild the famous café that burnt down, an ice cream van is usually there in summer – especially on weekends); Garrigill (mains-water pump to refill water bottles, free public toilets, pub, the post office shop has disappointingly limited wares and is not open Saturday afternoon or on Sunday); Nenthead (free public toilets, superb café, shop selling hot drinks etc., pub, bike repair centre).
Intermediate distances	Penrith, 7 miles; Langwathby, 12 miles; Hartside Top, 23 miles; Garrigill, 30 miles; Nenthead, 34 miles.

Tremendously hard and brilliant in equal measure, this day – which leads over several of the highest roads in England – is truly one of the great cycle tour experiences. It will live long in the memory. Starting off fairly innocuously along country lanes, the ride soon leads through a boarded-up red sandstone college, which very much evokes a feeling of having wandered onto the set of a last man on Earth dystopian film. Penrith is negotiated quickly and with little entanglement; it delivers a healthily tricky and enjoyable escape climb up Fell Lane and over Beacon Fell. Langwathby, in the Eden Valley, has a conveniently timed shop and is a great place to refuel and take stock before the big climbing into the Pennines really gets underway. The ascent to Hartside Top from Langwathby comes in three distinct phases. The first climb through Little Salkeld tops out near the Long Meg and her Daughters stone circle just off-route – well worth a visit. A second less severe climb is made over Viol Moor and from Renwick the great Hartside Top climb begins in earnest; it is long and unfurls varied passages of climbing before a gradual final 2km on the A road to the top.

A fast descent from Hartside is followed by undulating terrain leading to the isolated village of Garrigill where the C2C is crossed by the Pennine Way. On the approach, a clear view is had of the 'I hope it does not go up that' wall of tarmac that awaits riders on Flinty Fell. This needs to be overcome to reach Nenthead, and although it is jolly hard, is not as hard as it looks. A good, if difficult, off-road option also exists. From Nenthead, which generally serves as a well-needed place to recover and refuel, the route climbs to the glorious summit of the C2C on Black Hill at a dizzying 609m. Beyond this, a superb road with one more climb leads to Allenheads – which along with Nenthead is one of England's highest villages.

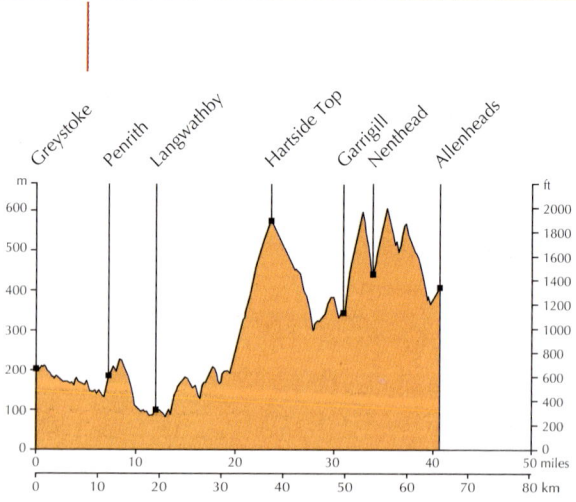

DAY 2 – GREYSTOKE TO ALLENHEADS

Having descended into the centre of **Greystoke**, a left is taken at the cross on the village green. This is signed to Great Blencow. Continue, despite a momentary disconcerting lack of signage, to pass Blencow Hall in 1 mile. Head directly through **Blencow** until a right is taken 400m later (the C2C now follows the 7 rather than the 71). The way leads through **Laithes** to **Newton Reigny** (pub), where a sharp left bend in the road turns riders eastwards. Shortly afterwards, a private road left turn is taken just after a metal C2C steel mile marker. This leads up through Newton Rigg and the grounds of a presently-closed red sandstone college. Creep over the brow of this eerie place then descend on a track that swings into a tunnel under the M6. Turn right after the tunnel and follow another private road, which soon crosses the West Coast Mainline, taking care with a section of bumpy churned-up concrete before reaching **Penrith**.

The ruined 14th century castle (free) at **Penrith** is testament to the town's turbulent history as a site of border raids by William Wallace and Robert the Bruce. Viking associations abound here too;

Penrith's ruined medieval castle has associations with Richard III

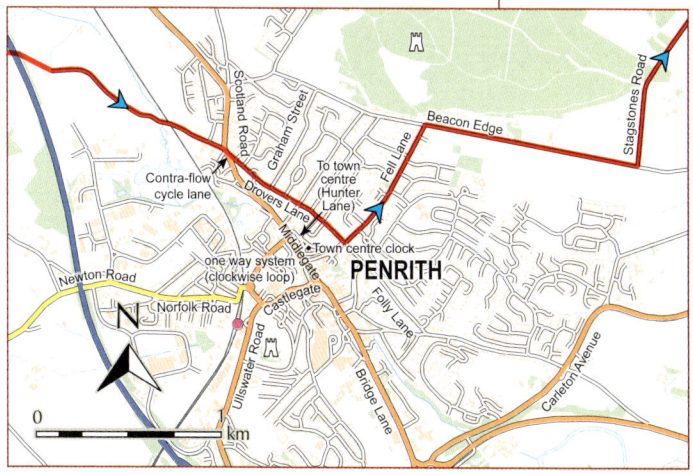

THE COAST TO COAST CYCLE ROUTE

the Norse Giant's Thumb monolith in St Andrew's churchyard is just off route. Penrith's lively town has a good selection of amenities. On the route out of the town, the strenuous Beacon Fell woodland area has a large hidden monument built in 1719 on the site of a beacon which warned of raids by the Scots. This can be visited by a short walk uphill from the junction at the top of Fell Lane.

At the T-junction, look out for a section of cycle path across and slightly rightwards – this is a contraflow cycle path. Use it, ignoring the no entry road signs that do not apply to cyclists and follow the cycle path – with care – down the hill. Heading over a first mini roundabout, continue straight on until eventually a set of two mini roundabouts is reached. Here, a left should be made up Fell Lane. ◀ At the top, turn right along Beacon Edge to

> Fell Lane is a reasonably tough climb, although the road is usually quiet and double yellows throughout ensure a generally good riding experience.

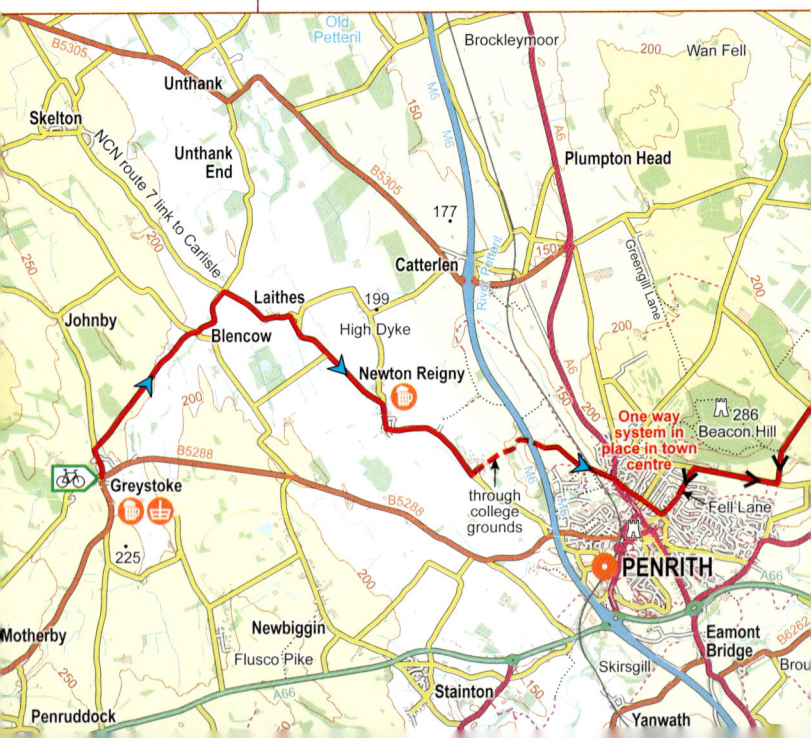

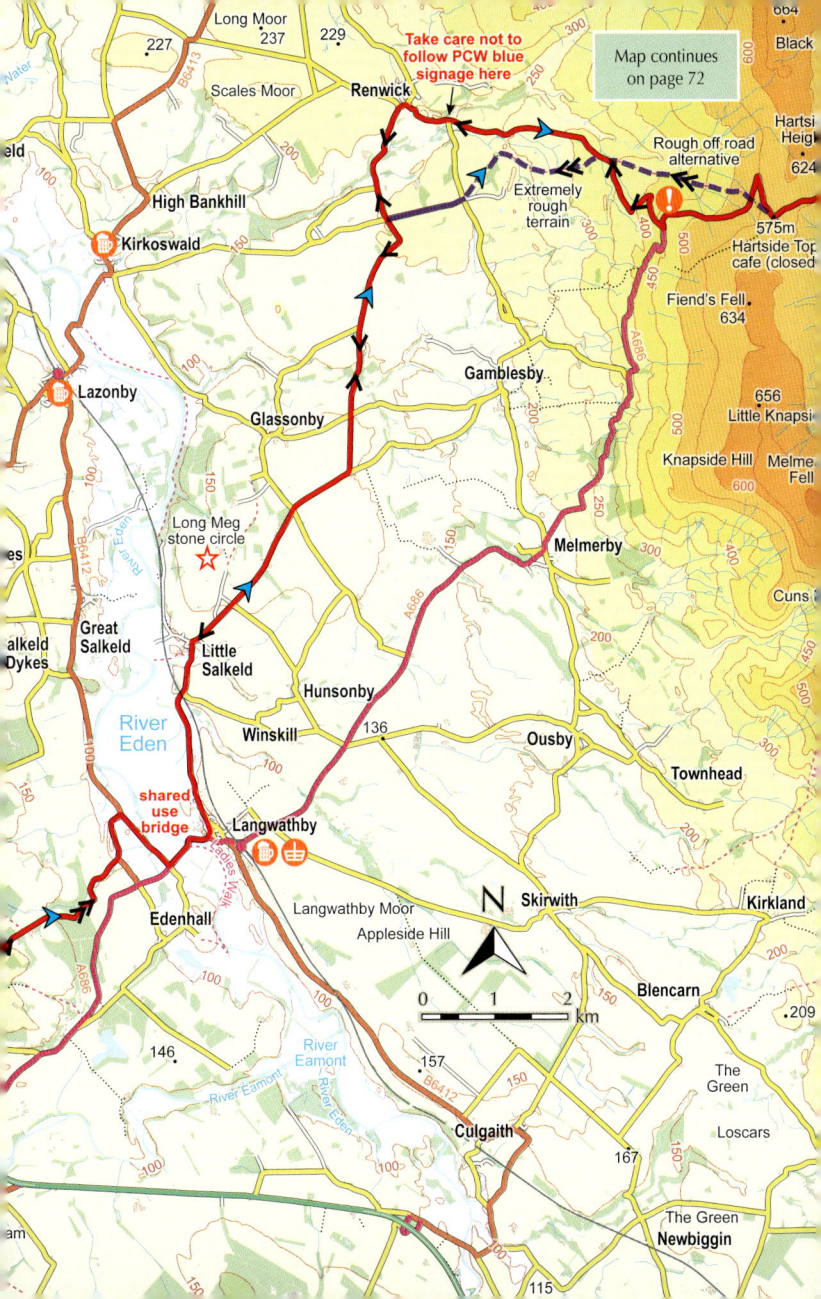

climb steadily with views of the Lakes on the right. A 200m descent is made from the brow, before a left turn is taken to climb over the shoulder of Beacon Fell.

A fast and steepening descent now ensues. This requires a degree of care, especially in the lower reaches where it snakes through trees. The hill somewhat spits riders out with speed onto a seemingly innocuous flat road with a clear sharp left bend ahead – be warned, there is nearly always accumulated loose sand and gravel at the bend. At the T-junction, turn left. After a further 400m, turn right off a bend and continue to the A road into Langwathby. Turn left on this and adopt the shared-use path on the left of the steel-meshed bridge to cross the River Eden. A brief climb brings riders to **Langwathby** village green – where a left (effectively straight on) is taken. This swings leftwards round the green, passing the local shop, which sells hot drinks – a last chance to refuel before the series of climbs that culminate in the epic Hartside Top ride are begun.

Long Meg and her Daughters

Long Meg and her Daughters is a stone circle created around 3500 years ago. Long Meg is the red sandstone monolith with mysterious carvings standing outside the circle of her daughters. The stones are reputedly a family of witches who were petrified as a punishment for dancing on the Sabbath. In a similar vein to the legends of Castlerigg, the circle's magic will break if anyone can count the same number of stones twice. The circle has a brooding backdrop of the **Cross Fell** group of the Pennines and is worth the short signed detour off the main route to visit. Cross Fell, which can be seen from the route throughout the Eden valley and the climbs beyond Garrigill and Nenthead, is the highest point in the Pennines. It is also the highest summit in England outside of the Lake District and the highest point of the Pennine Way at 893m. The notoriously bleak and blustery Cross Fell area even boasts its own wind, The Helm Wind, which sometimes produces a spooky shrieking noise in the vicinity.

DAY 2 – GREYSTOKE TO ALLENHEADS

On the longest climb of the ride up Hartside Top

Follow the road round to climb steeply through **Little Salkeld**. ▶ Take the second right off the bend at the offset crossroads – effectively straight on – signed Alston by a traditional finger post. Turn left on the descent, then take care heading straight on at the next crossroads. A punchy climb rears up after crossing Glassonby Beck to begin the ascent of Viol Moor. At the crossroads, riders have two options.

Road option
For the primary road option, descend straight on from the crossroads and cross Raven Beck where another

At the brow of the hill, riders have the option of turning left to visit Long Meg and her Daughters stone circle, ¼ mile away – return to route the same way.

Climbing up Hartside Top

feisty climb rears up. At **Renwick** the great Hartside climb begins in earnest and a right is taken. However, 500m later ensure you head straight on, following the 7 and ignore the blue 68 cycling sign pointing right, this catches the eye on a fast descent and riders have been known to go wrong here. The climbing now tests cyclists more by way of its ongoing nature than as a result of its steeper passages. Farmland gives way to untamed moorland, before a set of two long switchbacks weave through the hardest passage of climbing and a T-junction with the A Road is met. Turn left. Midweek riders may find the following 2km reasonably quiet, while weekend riders, especially on Sundays, may find they have to put up with tedious petrolhead motorbikers making lots of noise. Fortunately, the top is soon reached.

Off-road option

Alternatively, the horrifically rocky first stage of a three-stage unsurfaced off-road option can be taken. Turn right along the road and in 1km reach Five Lane Ends (anyone having second thoughts should escape left towards Renwick and rejoin the road route). Take the track uphill, directly opposite the junction. This frustrating, gruelling and slow-going track starts out rocky and uneven, before deteriorating into a disjointed boulder-strewn grind – bike-pushing is almost inevitable. On meeting the road option, turn right. Those masochists still up for the fight can now continue the off-road action by turning left in 300m onto a challenging bridleway. This can be a muddy and boggy affair. After passing a farm building, it emerges at the A road. The gravel track directly opposite is steeper than the gradual nature of the A road, but might be worth adopting.

> In the parking area at **Hartside Top** it is easy to make out the foundations of the well-loved former café, which burnt down in 2018. Before its fiery demise, the café laid claim to being the highest in England. At the time of writing, plans for a new café on the site were underway.

Approaching Renwick and the imposing climbs to come

THE COAST TO COAST CYCLE ROUTE

Main route

From Hartside Top descend for an extremely fast 3 miles on the A road, taking care with any cross winds as it is not uncommon to clock up 40mph. Be well-prepared to escape carefully onto the first right turn. This leads down a steepening minor road to a brake-burning T-junction at the foot of a 1 in 5 in the hamlet of **Leadgate**.

Alternative via Alston

Although off the official primary route, the attractive town of **Alston** sees a number of C2C cyclists making use of its accommodation and facilities and Sustrans have awarded it an alternative loop. The

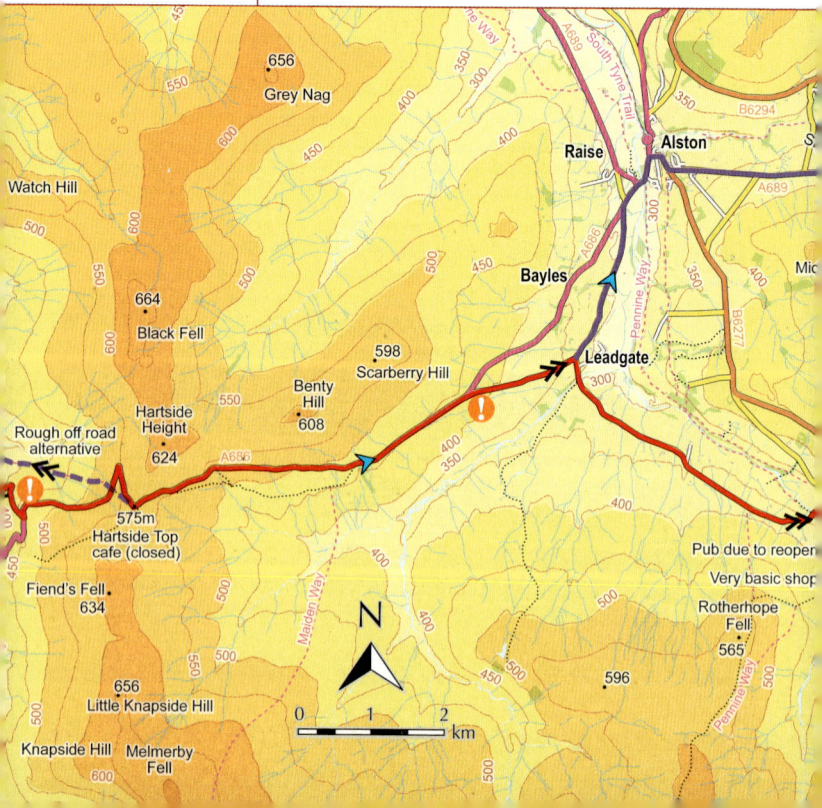

Day 2 – Greystoke to Allenheads

town is the start point of the South Tynedale heritage steam railway, which cyclists might hear tooting away nearby. In recent times, Alston was in the news with its plea for more women to come to the town – apparently males outnumbered females 10 to 1... they might come steaming in on the railway, or perhaps not.

A left at the T-junction in Leadgate leads straightforwardly with a final section on an A road to **Alston** in two miles. After crossing Alston Bridge and passing a petrol station, a steep right turn is taken uphill into the village centre (there are public toilets at the foot of the hill just before the turning). Sustrans have suggested using the easily

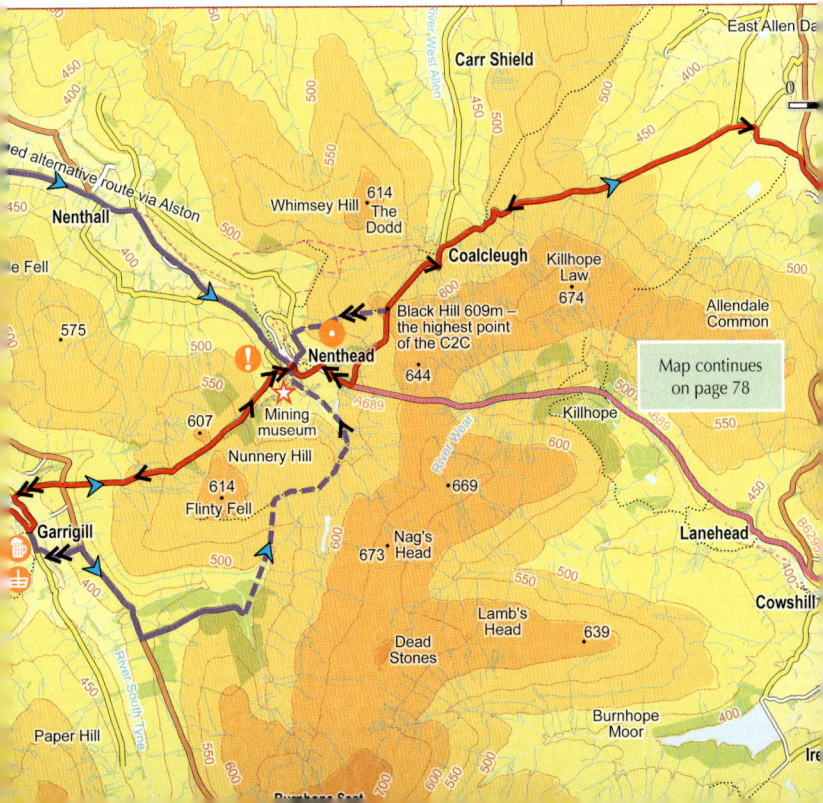

On the superb descent to Leadgate

In Garrigill free public toilets (water pump opposite) are at the village hall/ bunkhouse to the left of the George and Dragon Inn.

followed but massively disappointing A689 to reconnect with the primary route in **Nenthead**. We strongly recommend that if staying in Alston, cyclists accept they are on a spur and retrace the two miles to Leadgate, rather than make use of the demoralising A road to Nenthead. After all, it would be a great shame to miss out Garrigill and its famous climb.

Main route

In **Leadgate**, turn right downhill to find the road soon rears up after the bridge to an unwelcome 1 in 6. Beyond this, the way undulates while offering good views and eventually delivers riders to the remote village of **Garrigill**. ◀

> **Garrigill** feels remote, but it sees the crossing over of the C2C and Pennine Way. The historic George and Dragon Inn should reopen by Easter 2023. The village post office has limited wares and opening hours. There is an unlikely, yet brilliant, wrought-iron mains water pump to refill bottles directly opposite the toilets (ensure legs are spread wide,

Day 2 – Greystoke to Allenheads

the water comes out fast!). The nearby Yad Moss boasts the longest ski lift in England, while the impressive Ashgill Force – visited by the unsurfaced off-road option – is well worth a stop.

At the village green facing the George and Dragon riders have two options.

Road option
The road option heads left gently through the edge of the village, before a sharp right announces a gulp-inducing gradient shift. No sense burning out on this, it is wise to click quickly down into your lowest gear before beginning the fight for survival! This passage of straight 1 in 4 is comfortably the steepest of the entire C2C road route and sees many riders – especially the heavily-loaded – drop off into bike-pushing. However, those with hill experience and unrelenting tenacity can rest assured that once the 1 in 4 section is overcome, the gradient relents considerably and it is very easy to recover and settle into a rhythm on the long, but gradual enough, climbing to

Not the first cyclists to push up the steep climb out of Garrigill

the top. Thereafter, care is needed on the descent down Dowgang Hush to **Nenthead**. This mirrors the ascent in having a brakes-taxing 1 in 4 towards the bottom. Take care at the abrupt junction and swing rightwards to the centre of the village.

Off-road option

This off-road option is a hard one to fathom: the initial 400m section from **Garrigill** to the B2677 is firmly for masochists only, but the continuation is utterly delightful and affords the opportunity to see more of the Nenthead mines. The best option might be to experience the steepest road climb on the C2C, taking the normal 1 in 4 Garrigill climb to reach the B2677 and then head right along that for a mile to the start of the worthwhile off-road section. However, those determined to see how bad the first 400m are should part from the road route at Garrigill village green and head straight on for 100m, then take a left turn on an immediately rubbly track down to a bridge across the River South Tyne. The track then climbs shockingly steeply on boulders; it would be extremely challenging for a strong mountain biker to ride without pushing. The gradient eases and the rubble becomes tarmac after 400m. Carry on steeply uphill to reach the B2677. Turn right on this for 1km crossing a bridge directly above Ashgill Force en route. ◄ A clearly signed left at Mid Ashgill up a dead end road is now taken. The easy-going climb follows Ash Gill and eventually continues through Ashgill Wood. Descend to cross a charming cobbled ford then climb steeply to reach the end of the tarmac at Priorsdale Farm. Continue on loose but not overly rough track to easily gain the 547m high point of the climb, then swoop all the way down to Nenthead. The descent follows the mini valley of Old Carr's Burn; avoid gaining too much speed on the great section down to the mining levels as there are a few gravelly bends. The track splits just above the bottom Nenthead mine buildings. Unfortunately, the rubbly left branch must be taken here and most people will

It is worth going through the gate on the south side of the bridge to see the impressive waterfall.

want to wheel their bike down for around 50m. The centre of **Nenthead** with its enticing café is reached in a further 100m or so.

From the centre of Nenthead, there are two options to reach the high point of the C2C.

NENTHEAD

The village of Nenthead has a fascinating history

Although the route drops down dramatically into Nenthead, the village still lays claim to be the highest in England. The road route enters the formerly important mining village via Dowgang Hush – a hush being a channel where water was released to reveal mineral veins by stripping away soil. The off-road route rides right through the old silver, zinc and lead mine workings above the mining musem. Nenthead has an amazing history: it was the first purpose-built industrial village in England, formed by Quaker industrialists in 1704. The village had compulsory free schooling, public baths and the first free library in England. The Quakers' experiment was a huge success and the mines prospered; Nenthead even became the first UK village to have electric street lighting. Modern Nenthead is no less appealing – most C2Cers stop off here, if only to visit the excellent Hive café and gallery in the lovely former chapel. The Nenthead Mines Heritage Centre has a bunkhouse and organises underground tours through the extensive tunnels and panning for minerals.

The Coast to Coast Cycle Route

Road option

The road route starts off on the main road to Stanhope and climbs fairly steeply for 1.2km until a left turn is taken into wilder moorland terrain. The gradient eases here, but the climbing continues to the summit. At 609m – this is the fifth-highest road in England.

Off-road option

If the overview of this in the Unsurfaced off-road options section has not put you off, then take the road between the café and shop at **Nenthead**, climbing steeply at 1 in 5 over a short cobbled section. Straight after a short flatter section through Whitehall, turn right on a loose and awfully rough track which climbs unremittingly steeply up to reach the road route at Black Hill after 1km – expect some bike pushing.

Nearing the high point of the C2C at Black Hill on the track from Nenthead

Main route

From the Welcome to Northumberland sign on top of Black Hill, descend sweepingly for 1 mile before taking a right turn to commence the final climb of the day. The way now winds majestically over the wonderfully named Shivery Hill, 569m. Towards the bottom of the following long fast descent the road swings rightwards before dropping down to cross Middlehope Burn. At the T junction, turn right and roll steadily into the centre of **Allenheads** (pub, café/shop complex, free public toilets) to conclude a magnificent, if hard won, day's cycle-touring.

> **Allenheads** was a thriving lead mining village until 1896 and, somewhat bizarrely and after 80 mine-less years, it had a brief spell in the 1970s as a fluorspar mine. Evidence of both mining ventures is visible as you ride into the village and the small heritage centre is usually open and free to visit. As well as informing about the mining community, this houses an Armstrong hydraulic engine which was used in the mine's sawmill. Fans of winter sports may be surprised to learn that Allenheads still has a fully functioning micro ski resort, with two drag lifts open when there's sufficient snow.

EAST TO WEST

The signage is generally good in this direction. However, extreme caution is needed at the sharp right turn off the A road while descending from Hartside Top – it is unwise to try arm signalling here as you will probably need both brakes. As with the west–east option, ensure the left on the 68 is not mistaken for the C2C – it flashes up in a dip on the minor road section of the Hartside Top descent. Extra care needs to be taken escaping Penrith – especially where it is important to head straight on at the top of Drovers Lane in order to cross the A6 with a left (effectively straight on) onto Robinson Street just above the petrol station. On nearing Great Blencow, near Greystoke, the C2C leaves the NCN 7 in favour of a left turn onto NCN 71, which it then follows to the coast.

After leaving **Allenheads**, the climb over Killhope Moor proves direct and fairly sustained, while conversely the intermediate descent feels disappointingly less-protracted than its west–east counterpart. In consolation there is a free-flowing descent from Black Hill – although care needs to be taken on nearing Nenthead. The opening 1 in 4 out of **Nenthead** is hard, but not as hard as its opposite number coming west–east from Garrigill. The overall climb from Nenthead is less-protracted and therefore steeper, but the reward is a more gradual descent – at least, until the brake-burning caution required on the 1 in 4 near the village. The 1 in 5 out of **Leadgate** is an inauspicious opening to the long ascent of Hartside Top. Thankfully, this gradient soon eases; although it remains hard going to the A road. Unfortunately, the 3 miles gradually uphill on the A road to Hartside Top – which fly by west–east – prove demoralising, especially if faced with unfavourable winds and are unquestionably the biggest disincentive to an east–west crossing.

DAY 3
Allenheads to Tynemouth

Start	Allenheads (NY 860 453)
Finish	Tynemouth (NZ 374 691)
Distance	52 miles (83km)
Total ascent	845m
Steepest climb	Crawleyside Bank includes a passage of sustained 1 in 5 that bites.
Terrain	Minor roads and B roads before an impressive 35 miles on surfaced and unsurfaced cycle paths. Unsurfaced off-road option from Rookhope to Parkhead.
OS maps	Landrangers 87 and 88
Refreshments	Stanhope (pub on route and shops, cafés, bakery etc. just off-route); Parkhead Station (café – closed Mon–Wed, closes 3pm Thurs–Fri, 4pm on weekends). No simple access to cafes or refreshments until Land of Oak and Iron Heritage at the distant end of the Derwent Walk Country Park (7 days café, open till 4pm). Newcastle-Tyne Bridge waterfront area (pubs, cafés); The Hub – café.
Intermediate distances	Rookhope, 6 miles; Stanhope 10.5 miles; Parkhead Station, 13 miles; Consett 24.5 miles; Rowlands Gill 31 miles; River Tyne 36 miles; Newcastle – Tyne Bridge waterfront, 40 miles; The Cycle Hub (cycle repair) 41 miles, Segedunum Roman Fort, Wallsend, 44.5 miles.

With an impressive 35 miles or so of downhill or flat cycle paths on reclaimed rail lines to reach the sea from the remote Parkhead Station, the logic of Sustrans ending the flagship C2C in Tynemouth is not difficult to understand. With increasing access to such cycle paths throughout the UK over the past thirty years, it is easy to forget what a refreshing opportunity to escape the road network this once presented. However, after the mammoth Day Two, on-road cyclists will still need to test their mettle on three challenging climbs before they can glide effortlessly to the sea. The initial climb out of Allenheads is enjoyable and evokes a sense of the alpine before topping

THE COAST TO COAST CYCLE ROUTE

out at a beehive 'currick' (cairn) marking the gateway to County Durham – 'Land of the Prince Bishops'. An incredible 4½ mile freewheeling descent to Rookhope follows. From here, unsurfaced off-road cyclists on appropriate bikes should trade the two challenging road climbs via Stanhope, for one challenging – though mostly gradual – hill climb via Bolts Law Standing Engine to Parkhead Station. Those on road bikes need to tackle the excellent although testing minor road climb over the southern shoulder of Crow Coal Hill to Stanhope. Thereafter, a moment should be taken to steel resolve for one last great effort in order to wrestle with another of the classic test-pieces of the route: Crawleyside Bank. Crawleyside Bank was used for the National Hill Climb Championships in 1984, which gives a clue to its nature. Peaking with a sustained straight section of 1 in 5, it is not a beast easily slain, but it does come in stages that allow for recovery and a steadily paced ride will see it overcome with great satisfaction. From the remote café and B&B complex of Parkhead Station, which was formerly a station on an improbably high mining railway, cyclists can relax and meander their way steadily to the sea.

From **Allenheads**, follow the road uphill round the bend and head straight on at the crossroads. The road soon steepens to a prolonged passage of 1 in 7 beside pine trees. At the forested hairpins, the gradient eases off

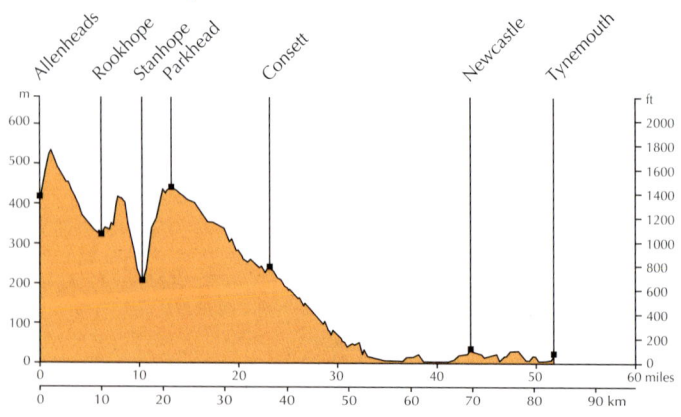

slightly and the beehive 'currick' (cairn) and open moorland at the top are soon reached. Continue to discover a descent that serves up 4½ miles of effortless cycling, passing some old mine workings and the **Rookhope Arch** before reaching **Rookhope**.

Shorngate Cross Currick marks the boundary between Northumberland and County Durham

The disused **Groverake Mine Buildings** can be seen beside Rookhope Burn. This was the last large scale **mine** in Weardale when it closed it 1999. A little further down the road, the Rookhope Arch once carried a 3km-long flue across the valley and up the hillside so that noxious lead smelting fumes could escape and valuable particles could be collected.

At the sharp bend and free public toilets in Rookhope, cyclists have two options.

Road option
Road bikes need to continue through the end of the linear Rookhope village then, after a 200m break in houses hugging the road, care needs to be taken not to miss a

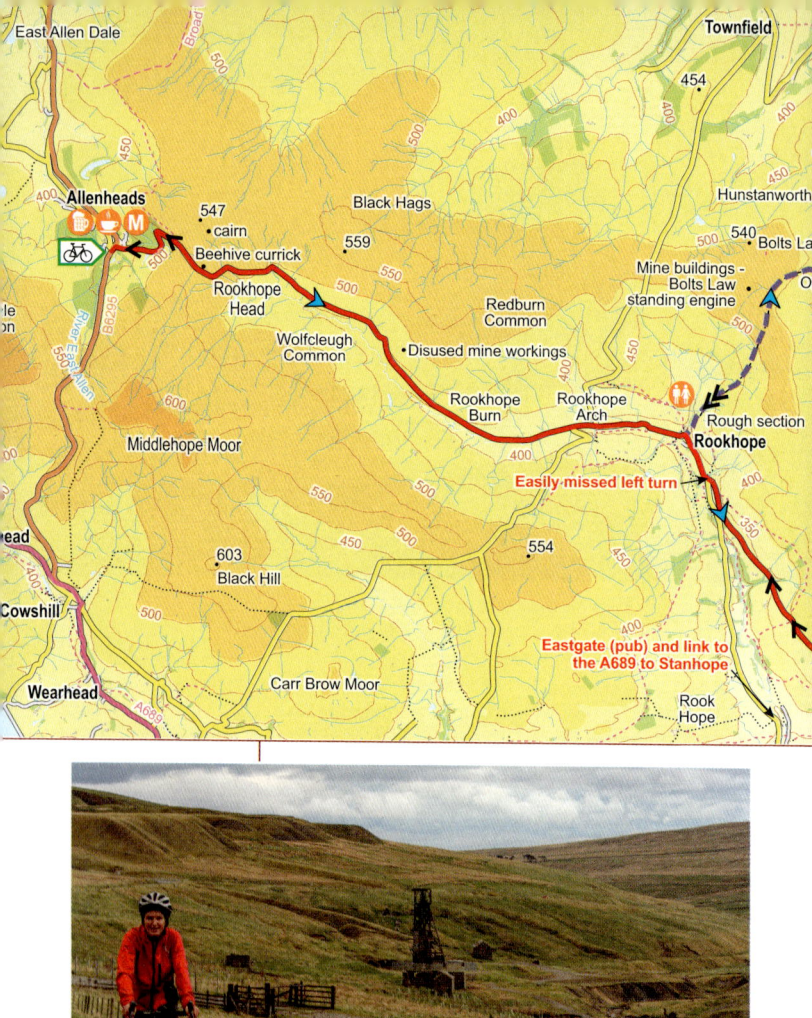

Groverake mine and the descent above Rookhope Burn

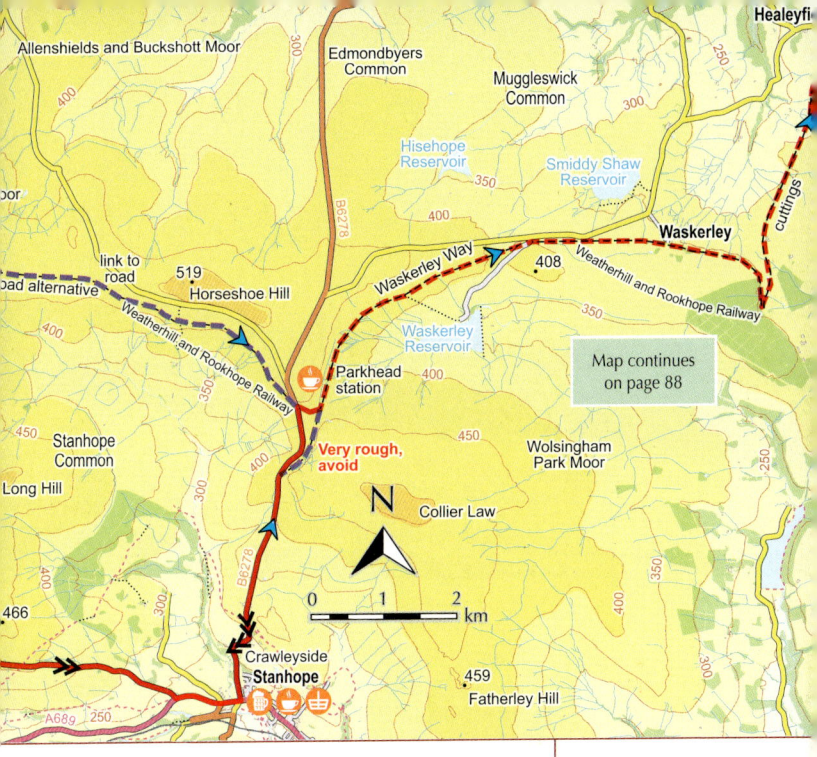

left turn onto a minor road uphill at a set of white-painted farmhouses. This road opens with a volley-shot of 1 in 6 before settling into an exceptionally quiet line that climbs in stages over the shoulder of Crow Coal Hill. Occasional steep passages appear, but overall this is highly scenic and enjoyable, giving views of the high expanse of Stanhope Common and the grand finale of the route up it. The descent into **Stanhope** is fast and requires care. Turn left at the A road to reach the turning for Crawleyside Bank at the Grey Bull pub, signed Edmundbyers (the centre of Stanhope with shops, cafés, bakery etc. is a further 600m or so along the A road).

Turn left and climb steadily at first. The road soon starts to rear up, but there is nothing that will cause undue concern until a sharp bend rightwards – that tellingly

Passing Waskerley Reservoir on a superb stretch of old rail path

has a sandbank escape lane for descending vehicles – announces a brutal 600m-long passage of sustained hard climbing. Steadier climbing follows for two miles until a right turn at an old railway mining carriage leads via several potholes to **Parkhead Station**.

Off-road option

Note: a sign will communicate if the moor is closed for grouse shooting.

Gravel bikes and hybrids should take the steep left turn up the gravel track off the bend in **Rookhope**. ◀ The surface of the track soon deteriorates to impart a brief spell of tricky technical riding up to a gate. Beyond the gate, the gradient eases and although Bolts Law Incline proves slow going on loose gravel, it is also a pleasant riding experience. An obvious cairn on the skyline signals the awaiting prize of the amazing flat terrain between Bolts Law Standing Engine and Parkhead Station.

From the remains of the impressive Bolts Law Standing Engine station (480m), the way is now more or less flat and arcs eastwards. Continue for 3km along the track to reach a fork. (The left-hand track leads easily over the brow of the hill to meet a road in 250m, which can then be taken rightwards to meet the B road just above the turning to Parkhead Station.) It is much better to continue on the former railway line despite the fact that it narrows into a pannier-teasing trough at times beyond the next crossroads. Near Parkhead, the path breaks up briefly and a little manoeuvring is needed, but nothing too annoying. A lovely raised section then brings Parkhead Station into view, where a descent onto the B road is followed by a right and left in quick succession to reach **Parkhead Station**.

> **Bolt's Law Standing Engine** once powered the highest-ever standard gauge railway in the UK. This was used to haul wagons laden with iron ore and lead to be smelted. Stanhope is a pleasant little market town with plenty of accommodation and an open-air heated swimming pool. It was the scene of skirmishes with invading Scots in the 14th century.

Main route

A gate at the rear of Parkhead Station commences the Waskerley Way. The gravel surface at the beginning of the trail is briefly disconcerting for those on road bikes, but all cyclists will soon discover they are making pleasingly rapid and easy-going progress on the former well-signed railway line. Progress is straightforward unless it is windy – a couple of minor roads are crossed here and there and the Way takes a somewhat disconcerting turn at a point where two old railway branch lines join and the route doubles back on itself for a few hundred metres, but is well signed.

Care should be taken crossing the A68 near **Rowley**. Thereafter, the Hownsgill viaduct is soon crossed by means of a churned up concrete surface.

> Although the **Hownsgill Viaduct**, completed in 1858, effects a sense of loftiness in C2C riders, the anti-suicide fences erected in 2012 after a high number of deaths unfortunately detract considerably from the aesthetic and diminish the ability

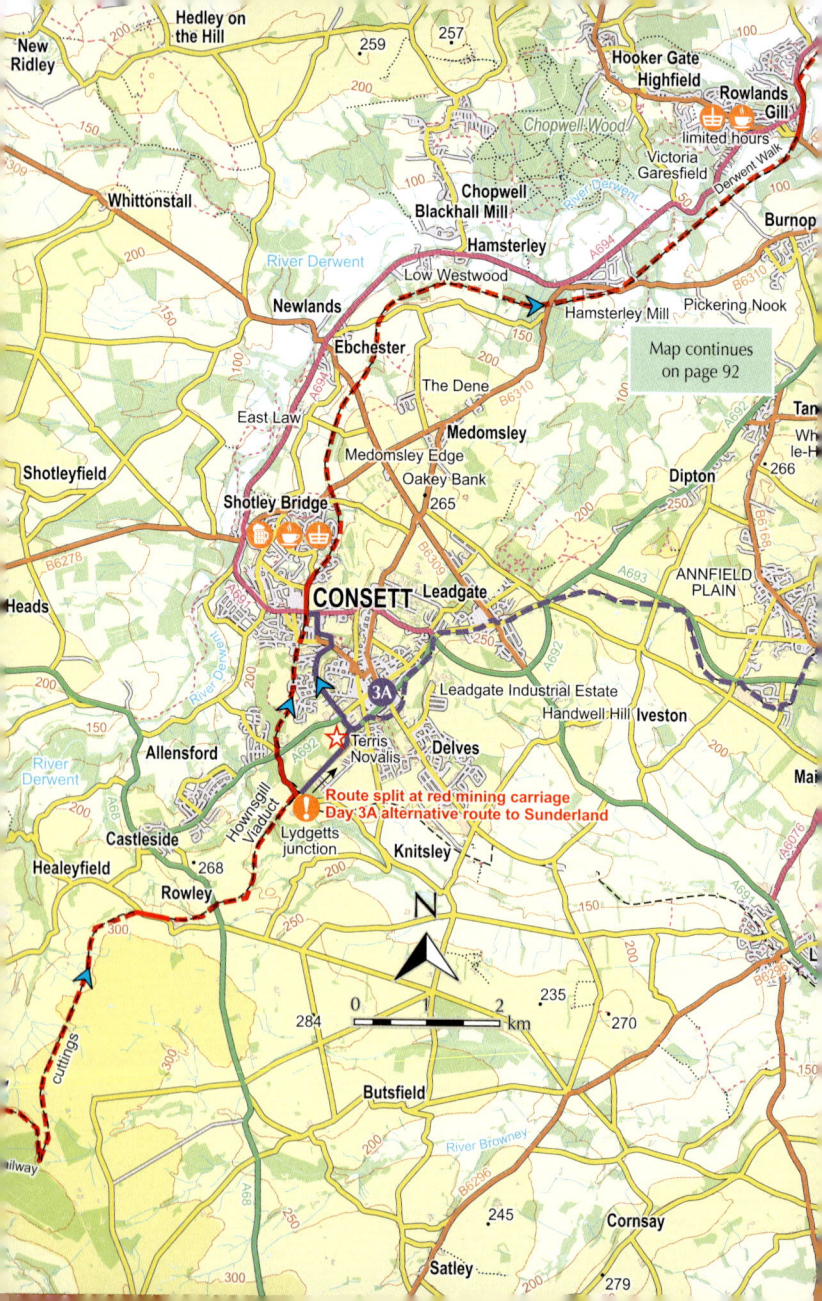

THE WASKERLEY WAY

Beware strong winds on the wide open Waskerley Way

The Waskerley Way is a superb 9.5 mile stretch of former rail track which runs from Parkhead station (café and accommodation) to Lydgetts Junction. Cyclists should keep their eyes peeled for slow worms and adders, which can be found on the extensive moorland. The line transported limestone and coal to South Shields until the 1960s. It originally operated by horse and gravity power, but latterly a standing engine at Hawkburn Head (the first parking area passed on route) did most of the work. The next parking and picnic area on route was once Waskerley Station – a thriving community with a school which became a ghost town after the closure of the lead mines and then the railway in 1969. A final picnic area before the viaduct was the old Rowley Station. This was dismantled and then painstakingly rebuilt brick by brick at the Beamish open air museum further along the route.

to comprehend the ridiculously impressive nature of this 46m high Victorian structure. It is worth taking time to peer down at the yawning ravine. Consett is a former steel town that supplied metal for the North East's shipbuilding industry. Most C2C cyclists have no reason to visit the town centre which is bypassed by the route, but several metal sculptures on the route hereabouts point to the town's heritage, including the unmissable red smelting wagon at Lydgetts Junction, where the two endings of the C2C diverge.

Roughly 400m after the Hownsgill Viaduct at **Lydgetts Junction** the key split in C2C options is marked by a giant red smelt wagon. (Those intending to finish in Sunderland should now refer to Day 3A.) Those intending to finish in Tynemouth have two options.

The majority of cyclists turn left downhill on the 14, where a right on a minor road is taken in 200m. After a further 200m, the cycle path can be accessed on the right. The A692 is soon reached and almost immediately afterwards a passage of uneven cycle path with a little access hill is introduced by a railway sleeper barrier. The well-signed cycle path, which follows the Derwent Walk at this point, now negotiates **Consett** with ease and leads on through the shady Byreside Woods near Hamsterley.

To visit the Terris Novalis sculpture

Riders have the option, however, of visiting the **Terris Novalis** sculpture, which is only 800m further along the cycle path from the smelt wagon. Although in theory it is possible to make a distinct connection to the Tynemouth route from here, it is actually much better and quicker to simply double back to the smelt wagon and follow the C2C to Tynemouth from there.

Main route

At **Rowlands Gill** the cycle path meets a road with a T-junction 20m to the right. It is easy to get disorientated here. Ensure you cross the road onto the shared-use cycle path. This is followed round the bend for 60m to a designated crossing that allows safe transfer onto the shared-use cycle path on the right hand side of the road. This shared-use path runs parallel to a B road for 350m, then parallel to an A road for a further 250m before an escape on the right can be taken onto the sheltered Derwent Walk.

Terris Novalis stands on the site of the Consett steelworks

The **Derwent Walk** is an excellent stretch of well-surfaced shared-use former railway path through lovely woodland scenery. This section of the route is an unexpected highlight on day three for many C2C riders. It includes the Nine Arches Viaduct, which was only built because a local landowner – the Earl of Strathmore – would not allow the railway to pass through his Gibside estate.

Immediately after crossing the 150m long **Nine Arches Viaduct** at Derwent Walk Country Park, a sharp left turn is taken to follow a circuitous 800m loop of a bend in the Derwent. As it loops back, an easily missed left turn is taken over a short bridge that takes riders onto the other side (north and west side) of the confusingly snaking River Derwent. Stay on this side of the river and continue along the cycle path. The open courtyard of the timber-clad and circular Land of Oak and Iron Heritage Building (café) will soon be seen on the left. The cycle path continues to take riders under the A1. Cut through

The iconic Tyne Bridge

by some allotments to run beside the Derwent and pass under another A road to reach a footbridge over the Derwent.

Confusingly, the footbridge rightwards is signed as the 'C2C Keelman's Way 14' – ignore this, it is an alternative option. (If you wish to take this somewhat frustrating route on the south side of the Tyne – see Keelman's Way option at the end of this chapter). Instead, pass under the footbridge and head leftwards on what is briefly the 141 link.

Follow the River Tyne upstream. As the route nears a green steel-latticed road bridge, a cycle ramp on the left is used to access the bridge. Cross over the Tyne by means of the shared-use path on the right-hand side and swing down to meet a cycle bridge, which is gained by a series of mind-bending gradual snaking ramps. Having crossed the bridge, Hadrian's Cycleway is met and a right turn is taken on a cycle path – now marked as NCN 72.

Day 3 – Allenheads to Tynemouth

When you reach the busy road, take advantage of the shared-use path for 100m or so before a pedestrian crossing takes you to the shared-use path on the river side of the road. Follow this for an awful 300m, until you can make a rightwards escape along the pavement of the quieter William Armstrong Drive. After 200m or so the path becomes a dedicated segregated shared-use cycle path beside the Tyne – thank goodness.

The **Newcastle** Quayside Path takes you into the heart of a cosmopolitan riverside area that is in turns vibrant and relaxing – many cycle tourers have been waylaid here on their way to the coast. Care can be needed with occasional blind turns, pedestrians, dog walkers and, on Sundays, a market where you have to dismount for 200m – a bell is of great help. The route is not difficult to follow and passes beneath the **Tyne Bridge** in two miles.

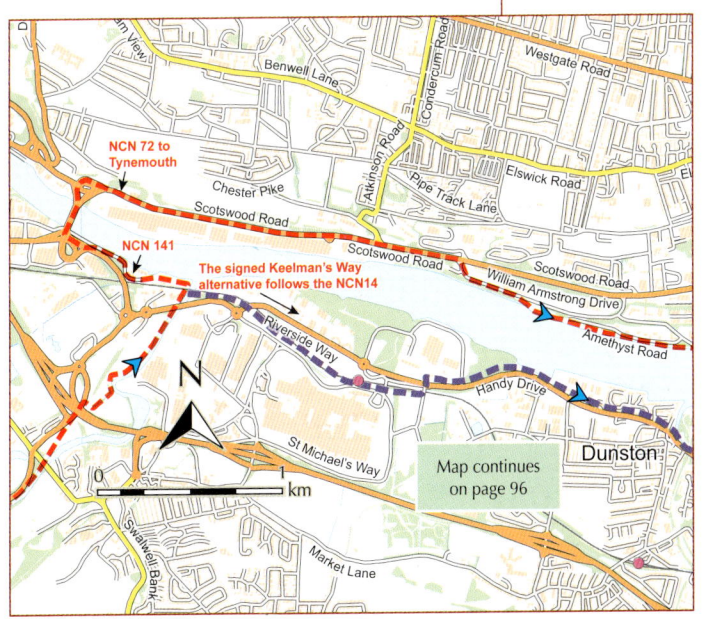

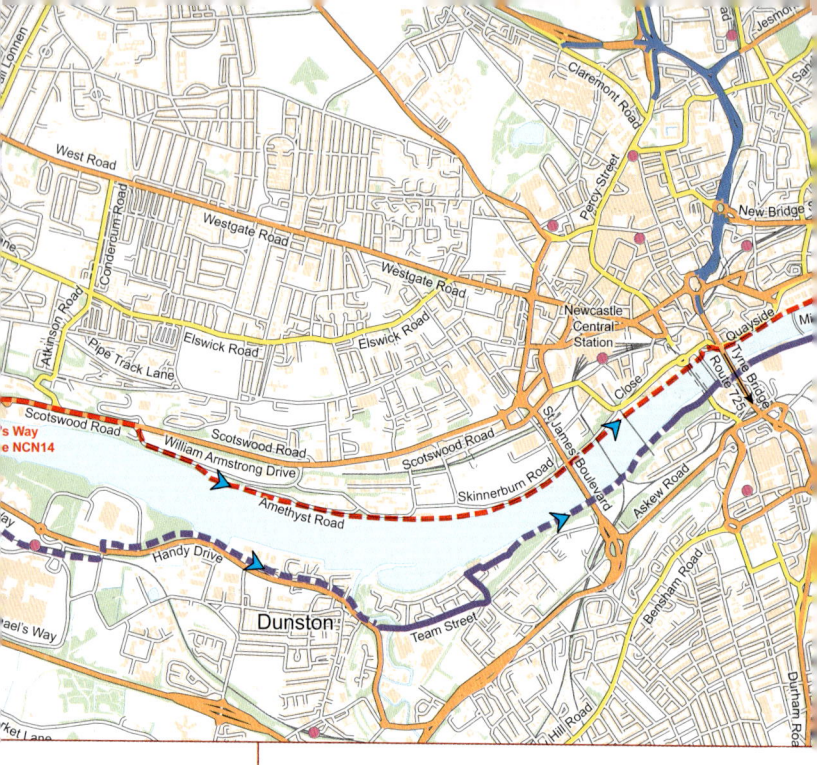

The iconic **Tyne Bridge** was opened in 1928 and was built by the same company that designed the Sydney Harbour Bridge. The Tyne Bridge is probably on the same site as Pons Aelius – the first bridge built across the Tyne by the Romans in the second century to serve the Pons Aelius Roman Fort. It is worth venturing onto the impressive full tilt Gateshead Millennium pedestrian and cycle bridge for good views.

Continue along the north bank of the Tyne. The cycle path ceases after a quay is crossed near 'The Hub' – a cycle hire shop, cycle mechanics and café that closes earlier than many running-late C2C finishers would like at 4pm. Continue on the left side of the surprisingly quiet

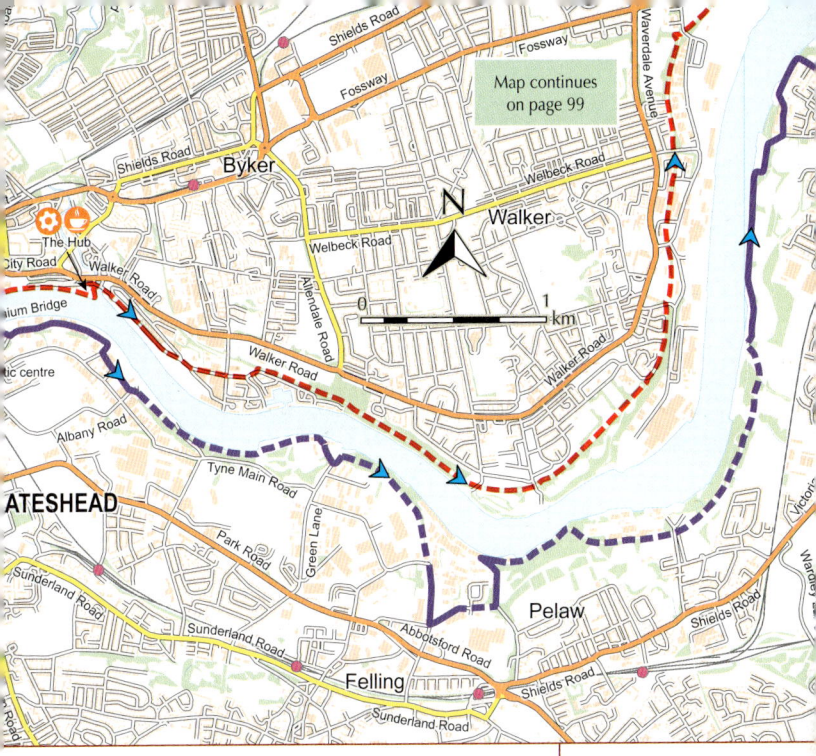

former industrial riverside road. As the road forks, bear left gradually uphill and across a mini roundabout. Bear left at the peculiar conjoined-twin Merman sculpture and in 60m take a left turn to access a cycle path that is followed rightwards.

This raised cycle path is shared with the Hadrian's Cycleway and Hadrian's Wall Path and follows a former rail line mostly through trees. It makes for pleasant quieter riding after the bustle of the quayside. There are five minor road crossings that interrupt the path before the **Segedunum Roman Fort** at **Wallsend**.

The end of Hadrian's Wall is a satisfying milestone, although there are five intricately worked miles still to wheel until the journey's end. These miles require diligent route finding. Continue along the segregated cycle

SEGEDUNUM ROMAN FORT

At Wallsend, an excavated section of Hadrian's Wall from the Segedunum Roman Fort is bisected by the cycle path. While this small section of wall is a little scruffy and invariably plagued by urban detritus – there is nonetheless something fascinating in seeing that its stone had been buried and not, over the centuries, entirely appropriated by urban developments. The stretch of wall that drops away from the path has a derelict office building on top of it and looks bizarre, although it was only in the 1970s that the fort was – somewhat surprisingly – revealed during the clearance of Victorian terraced housing. Segedunum was constructed between AD122–127 as an eastern extension of Hadrian's Wall from the Pons Aelius Fort. Although the ruins can mostly be seen from the perimeter, a small fee allows entrance to a museum and worthwhile viewing tower.

Note: the Tyne cycle and foot tunnel can be accessed by ignoring the path, turning left at the junction and continuing until 100m beyond the first roundabout a right turn is taken down Coach Open.

path; in 500m a special arch commemorates Hadrian's Cycleway. The roundabout beyond is initially negotiated on the right, but while a cycle path continues on the right-hand side of the road, it is necessary to cross over to the shared-use cycle path on the left side of the road. This parts company with the road completely by slipping leftwards downhill beside the Willington Viaduct where there are slightly different winding lines for uphill and downhill cyclists. Turn right on reaching Ropery Lane, then take a left after 50m or so onto an easily missed cycle path that sneaks past a small industrial estate. ◄

The path emerges on Armstrong Road, which you follow to its conclusion. Turn left and go round to the next junction where a left turn uphill is followed immediately by a right turn at a road crossing onto a cycle path. This weaves a little circuitously but brilliantly to cross a bridge over the A19 where the Tyne Tunnel will be seen. A first roundabout is largely negotiated by a cut-through cycle path on the right. Shared-use cycle paths on the right of the road lead to a third roundabout, where a right turn still on the shared-use pavement leads down Coble Dean at the Royal Quays. Look out for an easily missed left turn using a road crossing to a cycle path hidden in trees. This niftily runs through a series of small parks with monuments to reach the River Tyne Marina.

Day 3 – Allenheads to Tynemouth

The path turns sharply left at the Royal Quays Marina. Follow the water's edge for 200m until turning right across a small bridge and continue around the harbourside, past hundreds of sailing boats, to join a roadside cycle path up a short hill. At the top turn right and continue trending rightwards down through the new Smith Dock development to reach Fish Quay. (Note: a hidden right just after a mini roundabout leads to the Shields Ferry terminal to South Shields and the end of Hadrian's Cycleway). ▶

Fish Quay is the biggest prawn port in England.

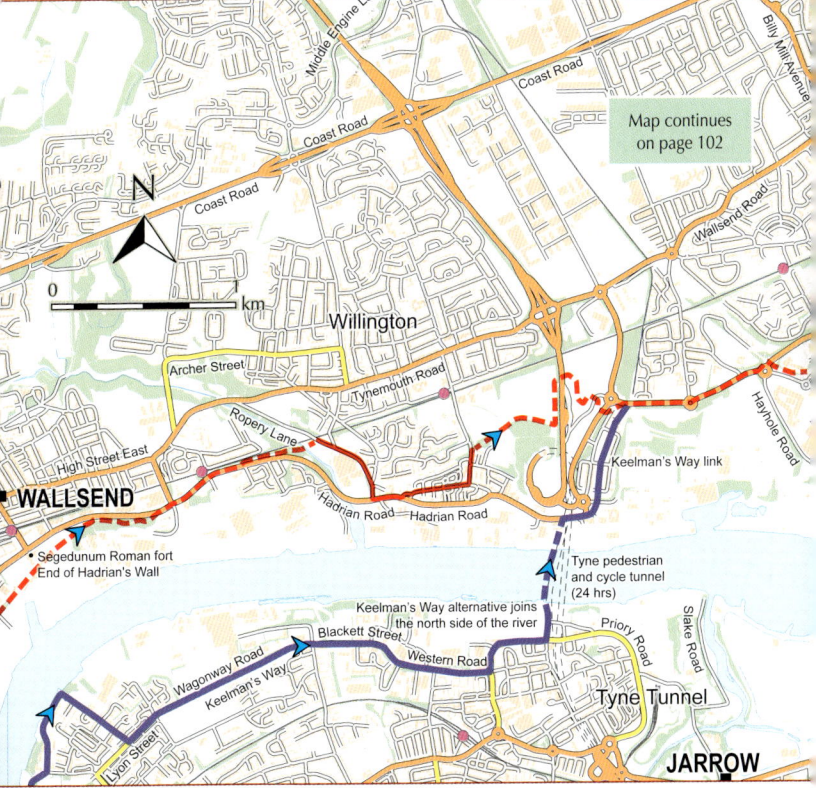

Tynemouth Priory and Castle above King Edward's Bay

Just after the white tower of the Fish Quay Low Light House (small museum with fee), turn right onto the quayside path, passing Clifford's Fort and soon reaching the sculpture of three giant buoys commemorating NCN 72 and Reivers Route 10 by a car park and public toilets. The harbourside path is then followed for the remainder of the route. The landmark of Tynemouth's Spanish Battery looms large and the open North Sea beckons beyond the river's mouth. Where the promenade ends, the path veers steeply up to a disappointing small finger sign – this is the official end of the route at **Tynemouth** – then tops out at some paid for car parks. However, surely such a momentous crossing of the country needs marking with a celebratory dip of feet, or wheel, in the North Sea. The small nearby bay, which is home to Tynemouth Sailing Club, is one option (free time-limited car park opposite the ramp). It is possible to access the path beneath the castle and follow the pier to reach the lighthouse – a great position. Alternatively, continuing up over the headland and past the impressive Tynemouth Castle and Priory, allows access to the steps down to the dramatic sweep of the lovely King Edward's Bay, just below the castle headlands.

Day 3 – Allenheads to Tynemouth

KING EDWARD'S BAY AREA

On this part of the route you will see a large **statue** of Lord Cuthbert Collingwood, who was Admiral Nelson's second in command at the Battle of Trafalgar. The treacherous **Black Middens rocks**, which wrecked five ships during three days of storms in 1864, lurk in the Tyne beside the route. The **Spanish Battery** being the raised area where the route ends is likely to take its name from Spanish mercenaries who defended Henry VIII's fleet from gun placements here. **Tynemouth Castle** stands proud upon the rocky headland. The castle boasts an impressive moat and ruined gatehouse and keep. The site also contains the ruins of the Benedictine **priory**, where two kings of Northumbria and one king of Scotland were buried. The site is thought to have been occupied since the Iron Age. The castle is now managed by English Heritage (fee to enter). **Tynemouth centre** is nearby and has a wide range of amenities.

BICYCLES ON THE METRO

Between 10am–3pm and after 7pm bikes are now allowed on the Metro rail network. The only catch is that the most central stops (such as the Metro for Newcastle Central Station) do not allow them. Therefore, you should get on the metro at Tynemouth (straight up Front Street from the castle, left at the top on Allendale Place, then right along Station Terrace) and disembark at Manors on the yellow line. From here it is about a mile to Newcastle Central rail station. From Manors Metro exit, go straight ahead, round the back of student accommodation, to find a cycle flyover of the A167M. Cross this and go left and left again onto Market Street, eventually picking up blue cycling signage that leads straight on through shopping areas to reach the main rail station.

Keelman's Way

The Keelman's Way is an inferior south side of the Tyne C2C approach that offers an alternative to the standard route. Although the Keelman's Way terminates at the shoreline in South Shields, for the C2C it is followed as far as the Tyne Pedestrian and Cycle tunnel. If you wish to continue on the South side of the Tyne on the Keelman's Way, now signed as NCN 14, the Cicerone webpage for this book has a full route description.

THE COAST TO COAST CYCLE ROUTE

Late finish at the end of the ride beneath the Spanish Battery

EAST TO WEST

Theoretically, the route finding is well-badged and should be straightforward leaving **Tynemouth** or **Sunderland** all the way to Parkhead. However, North East urban centres offer a complex of myriad cycle paths; careful route finding and a mind-bending reversal of the west–east description in this book may be required from either start until Lydgetts Junction just beyond Consett, where the C2C resolves itself into a less entangled affair. In order to cross the Tyne in **Newcastle**, cyclists need to look out for a left turn on the (14) – actually 141, and not continue to follow the 72 (HCW). This left gains a cycle bridge over a busy A road that involves a careful descent of an intricately-ramped tower. Once the Tyne is crossed by the segregated shared-use path on the left of the road, the route bears left back downstream and leads to a tunnel next to the River Derwent. It is vital that riders are prepared on emerging from the tunnel to follow the C2C 14 signed to Consett and ignore the 'C2C 14 Keelman's Way' (which is an alternative west-east finish that crosses the River Derwent via a footbridge). If going from **Parkhead** via Bolts Law Standing Engine to **Rookhope**, riders should not be demoralised by the awkward start to this section – it soon coalesces into an impressive high-level route. Those taking the road option must take considerable care on the steep arcing 1 in 5 descent of Crawleyside Bank. The final climb over to **Allenheads** beside Rookhope Burn is, for the most part, incredibly gradual, but conversely it is open to the elements and can be challenging if winds are not favourable.

DAY 3A
Allenheads to Sunderland

Start	Allenheads (NY 860 453)
Finish	Sunderland (NZ 408 589)
Distance	49 miles (79km)
Total ascent	822m
Steepest climb	Crawleyside Bank includes a passage of sustained 1 in 5 that bites.
Terrain	Minor roads and B roads before an impressive 35 miles on surfaced and unsurfaced cycle paths. Unsurfaced off-road option from Rookhope to Parkhead. Some rough cycle path into Sunderland.
OS maps	Landrangers 87 and 88
Refreshments	Stanhope (pub on route and shops, cafés, bakery etc. just off-route), Parkhead Station (café – closed Mon–Wed, closes 3pm Thurs–Fri, 4pm on weekends), Annfield Plain, Beamish, Washington Wetlands, Sunderland Glass Centre, Roker beach and pier area.
Intermediate distances	Rookhope, 6 miles; Stanhope 10.5 miles; Parkhead Station, 13 miles; Consett 24.5 miles; Stanley, 33 miles; Washington, 41.

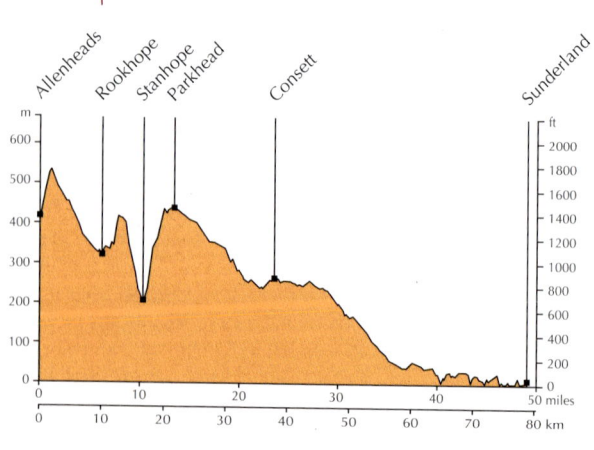

DAY 3A – ALLENHEADS TO SUNDERLAND

THE RAILWAY PATH SCULPTURES

The Consett to Sunderland Railway Path Sculptures liven up this 20-mile stretch of traffic-free path. Although they have become inevitably weather-beaten and suffered at the hands of graffiti artists, the chain of sculptures do bring the heritage of an area that was once an industrial powerhouse to life as you whizz by. First comes Terris Novalis – two huge stainless-steel sculptures of engineering instruments with animals' feet. The work is on the site of what was once the biggest steelworks in Europe. Near Leadgate is The Jolly Drovers' Maze. You would be forgiven for thinking this ridiculously twisting and turning section of route was some urban planner's idea of a joke; cyclists must ride at super-slow speed through the labyrinthine hummocky area, which supposedly replicates a maze of underground mining tunnels. At Pontop Pike are the Old Transformers: Miner and Ironmaster, which are rather like the famous heads of Easter Island. The sculptures are made from the recycled materials of old industrial transformers, used to connect the steelworks to the power grid. By the Beamish Museum are the Beamish Shorthorns, a group of cows sculpted from reclaimed heavy machinery. Further still down the route, King Coal looks out over several former mining communities. This huge sculpture is made from bricks and railway sleepers. The route also passes the Beamish Open Air Museum which shows visitors what life was like in the North East through history. Many original buildings were dismantled and rebuilt on site to create a station, colliery, pit village and tramway.

The Beamish Shorthorns are among many sculptures on the rail path

Follow Day 3 until **Lydgetts Junction**. From the red smelt wagon at Lydgetts Junction continue straight on to reach the **Terris Novalis** sculptures. After these, the track soon ends. Carefully follow cycling signage across the road to turn left but swing rightwards on the cycle path at the

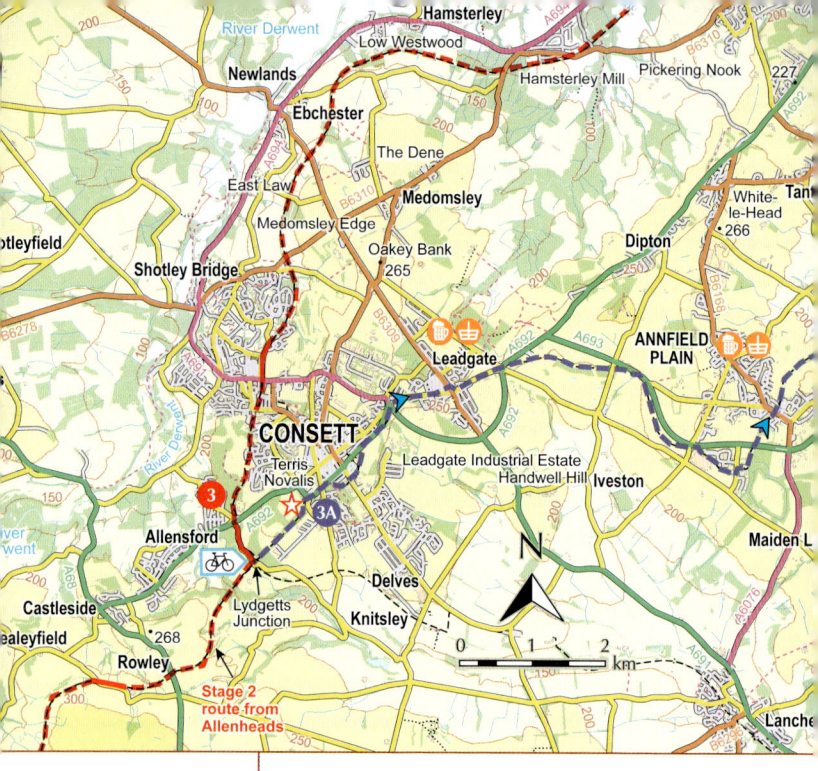

right of the A road for 100m before it escapes rightwards. A road is soon crossed and an awkward cycling gate is negotiated to enter a small park which avoids busier roads.

Cross another road with care, then look out for a left turn into the grounds of **Consett** football club. This section dodges a busy road but the surface is temporarily quite rough for road bikes. Eventually cross another large roundabout with care at a junction of A roads where there is a supermarket. Join a wide tarmac cycle path beside a road with signage announcing that you will be in Stanley in 27 minutes. Cross the road just after being welcomed to **Leadgate**. Dogleg left into a housing estate then look out for an easily-missed right turn onto a cycle path (not South Cross Street) leading along the back of houses with several

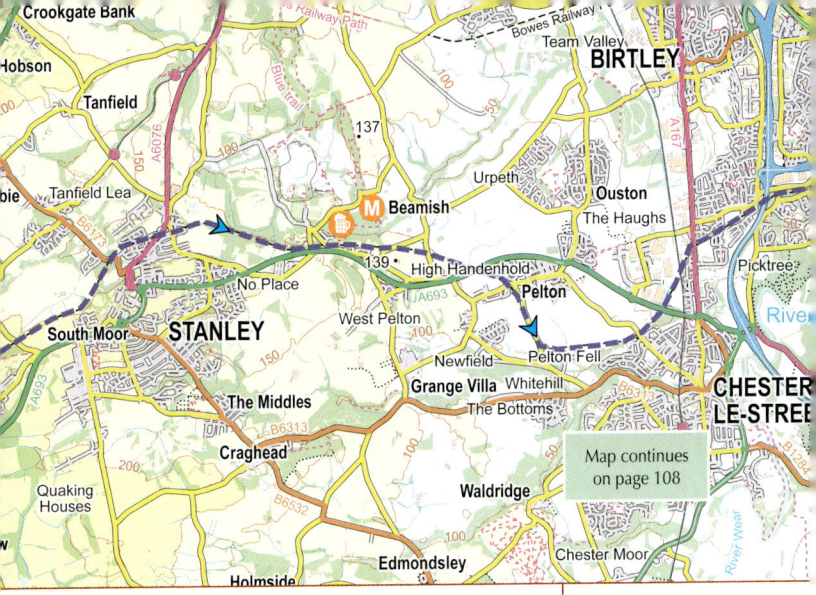

metal barriers designed to prevent motorbikes. Continue straight on, crossing a main road in Leadgate to soon reach a large final roundabout at the Jolly Drover pub. It is easy to go wrong here. Follow the shared-use path safely round the roundabout until, opposite to the pub, a wavy steel sculpture denotes the C2C. Care is needed as this path initially weaves very sharply through the Jolly Drovers Maze sculpture with its blind bends. The path soon becomes the Consett and Sunderland railway path and passes the Transformers sculptures, then briefly runs beside a main road before continuing easily but with a slight height gain. On the outskirts of Annfield Plain join a narrower cycle path past a gigantic wind turbine and then a fishing pond.

Where this path emerges at a small road, turn left then almost immediately right onto another cycle path. The next section through Annfield Plain is not perfectly signed, but the route heads straight on at any spots where there might be doubt and easily gets back onto the railway path to Stanley.

Stanley is bypassed with ease on a faster stretch of gravel and tarmac railway path with pleasant wooded

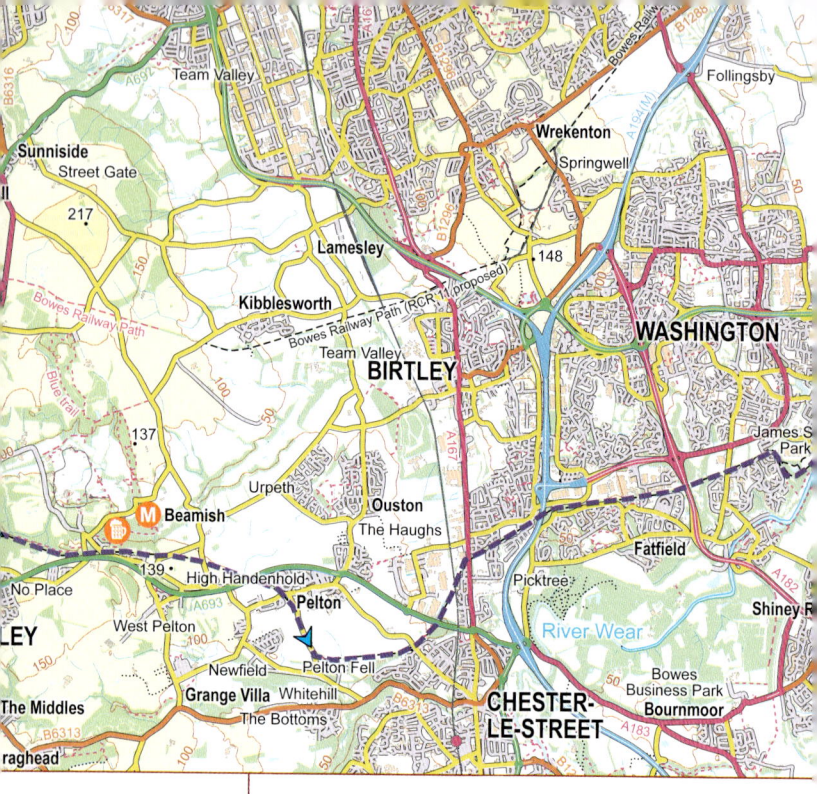

sections that include the series of metal cow sculptures. The route passes close by the Beamish open air museum and Lambton.

The **legend of the Lambton worm** tells of local man John Lambton's battle with a worm that he fishes from the River Wear. The worm grew to goliath proportions and terrorised the area, snatching local children, until the man eventually vanquished it with the help of a local witch. Unfortunately, as part of his deal with the witch, the curse of the worm was put upon many generations of Lambton's family. The fascinating aspect of this famous Sunderland myth is that many members of the Lambton family

really did go on to die in strange circumstances, adding credibility to the wicked worm's dreaded legend. The story is said to have inspired both Lewis Carroll's Jabberwocky and Bram Stoker's novel The Lair of the White Worm.

Continue easily for several miles towards the outskirts of **Washington**, going over the main rail line and under the A1. The route leaves the railway path at the James Steel Park woods, where the River Wear becomes visible in places, and shares a small section with the Teal Farm nature trail. This passage is less than ideal for road bikes, but is short-lived. Take care to follow C2C east signage at a wooded climb followed by a dip. Before the bottom, the C2C route branches left (before reaching the riverside) and rises to gain a quiet road. This joins a bigger roadside path and passes a sewage works. Head right at the roundabout on the cycle path, then take a left leading onto a minor road past the entrance to the **Washington Wetlands Centre** (café with views of the birds), then go right onto a cycle path.

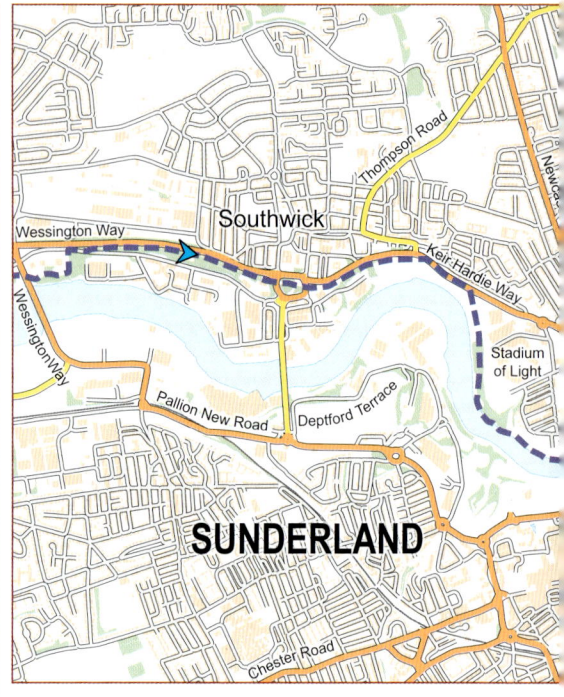

The **Washington Wetland Centre** is a series of lakes and a saline lagoon beside the River Wear. It is home to everything from otters to flamingos.

The first mile of path is unsealed, before a left then right turn leads onto a tarmac section, heading away from the River Wear and running parallel with the busy A1231 and A19 for about a mile. Breathe a sigh of relief as you turn sharply left under and away from the A19 with views of the widening Wear and the finishing strait lifting the spirits.

Briefly reach the river, then follow a lane uphill across and straight on to join a cycle path to your right on a banking. This eventually leads down to the Wear and the final 10km of the route is on good paths often

DAY 3A – ALLENHEADS TO SUNDERLAND

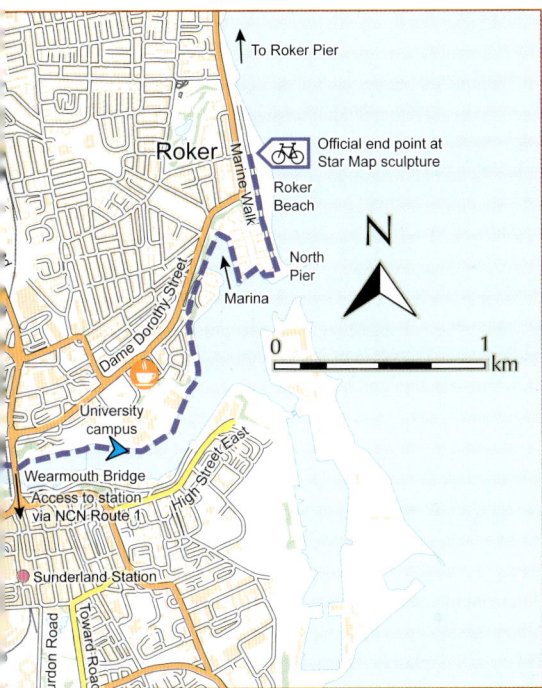

beside the river. Follow the Wearside path easily to the Wear suspension bridge.

Climb steeply to go under the bridge (keep on the cycle path to the right side of the road here). Continue climbing to join a road and take a segregated path to its right. After 1km, signs suggest two route options. Follow the riverside route by heading right downhill on the cycle path then turn left on Wayfarer Road to reach more cycle path leading to the Wear. The path sweeps brilliantly beside cliffs beneath Sunderland FC's **Stadium of Light**.

Shortly afterwards, pass under two distinctive road and rail Wear bridges into a nicely developed section past part of Sunderland University and the **National Glass Centre** (café), where there is a sculpture park.

> **Shadows in Another Light** is a sculpture of a tree in the shape of a hammerhead crane used in the Sunderland shipyards. The sculpture stands on the concrete former base of one of these cranes and various nuts and bolts from it are used in the artwork.
>
> The **National Glass Centre** features galleries of arty glass, glass-blowing demonstrations and a café.

There is a final rise to briefly join a road and then regain a delightful harbourside section of the path around the marina and North Pier to reach the official end of the route by the circular **Star Map sculpture** – which sees the Roker Pier lighthouse framed. A dip of the toe in the North Sea on the beach or a breezy jaunt along the cobbled **Roker Pier** to the lighthouse are optional.

> **Roker Pier** is a local landmark and acclaimed feat of Victorian engineering. Its distinctive stripy lighthouse can also be reached by an underground tunnel which enabled the lighthouse keeper to reach his post during inclement weather. Visitors can now pay for a tour to make a similar journey.

A glorious evening on Roker Beach after a successful one day C2C ride

The Star Map sculpture marks the end of the C2C

APPENDIX A
Accommodation

Location	Type	Name	Phone	Website or email	Evening meal available	Distance along route	Bike storage
Whitehaven	Hotel	Chase Hotel	01946 693656	chasewhitehaven.co.uk	Yes	0km	Yes
Whitehaven	Guest House	Glenard	01946 692249			0km	
Workington	B&B	Dower House Guest House	01900 605906	dowerhouse-workington.co.uk		0km alt	Yes
Workington	Pub	Waverley	01900 603246	waverley-hotel.com	Yes	0km alt	Yes
Loweswater	Pub	Kirkstile Inn	01900 85219	kirkstile.com	Yes	26km	Yes
Lorton	Pub, caravans, camping	Wheatsheaf Inn	01900 85199	wheatsheafinnlorton.co.uk	Yes	34km	Yes
Lorton/Scales	B&B	Swinside End Farm	01900 85134	swinsideendfarm.co.uk	At pub	34km	Yes
Lorton	Camping	Whinfell Hall Farm	07796976907	whinfellcampsite.co.uk	At pub	34km	
Cockermouth	Hotel	Manor House Hotel	01900 828663	manorcockermouth.co.uk	Yes	16km alt	
Cockermouth	B&B	Croft GuestHouse	01900 827533	croft-guesthouse.com	Nearby	16km alt	Yes

APPENDIX A – ACCOMMODATION

Location	Type	Name	Phone	Website or email	Evening meal available	Distance along route	Bike storage
Thornthwaite	B&B	Powter Howe	017687 78415		2 miles	43km off road alt or 40km +3km main route	Yes
Thornthwaite	Camping/pods	Lanefoot		stayinthornthwaite.co.uk	1.5 miles	as above	
Braithwaite	B&B/inn	The Coledale Inn	017687 78272	coledale-inn.co.uk	Yes	42km	
Braithwaite	Camping	Braithwaite C and C Club	024 7647 5426	campingandcaravanning-club.co.uk	At pub	42km	
Keswick	YHA hostel	Keswick YHA	0345 371 9746	yha.org.uk	Yes	48km	Yes
Keswick	B&B	Cranford House	01768 771017	cranfordhouse.co.uk	Nearby	48km	Yes
Keswick	Hostel	Denton House	01768 775351	dentonhouse-keswick.co.uk	Nearby	48km	Yes
Keswick	B&B	Grassmoor Guest House	01768 774008	grassmoor-keswick.co.uk	Nearby	48km	Yes
Keswick	B&B	Bluestones	01768 774237		Nearby	48km +500m	Yes
Keswick	B&B	HillCrest22 Guest House	01768 772179	hillcrest22keswick.co.uk	Nearby	48km	Yes
Keswick	Camping	Derwentwater C and C club	01768 772579	campingandcaravanning-club.co.uk	Nearby	48km	
Keswick	Camping	Castlerigg Farm	01768 772479	castleriggfarm.co.uk	Nearby	48km +1.5km	Yes

THE COAST TO COAST CYCLE ROUTE

Location	Type	Name	Phone	Website or email	Evening meal available	Distance along route	Bike storage
St John's in the Vale	Camping/glamping	Burns Farm	01768 779112	burns-farm.co.uk		55km alt or 55 +2km main	
Threlkeld	Pub	Horse and Farrier	01768 779688	horseandfarrier.com	Yes	55km	
Threlkeld	Pub	The Sally	01768 779614	thesalutation.co.uk	Nearby	55km	Yes
Mungrisdale	Pub	Mill Inn	01768 779632	robinsonsbrewery.com	Yes	61km	
Troutbeck	Camping	Gill Head	01768 779953	gillheadfarm.co.uk	Nearby	65km	
Troutbeck	Pub	The Troutbeck Inn	01768 489145	troutbeckinn.co.uk	Yes	65km	
Troutbeck	B&B	Lane Head Farm	01768 779220	laneheadfarm.co.uk	Nearby	65km	Yes
Scales	Bunkhouse/Pub	White Horse Inn	01768 779883	thewhitehorse-blencathra.co.uk	Yes	66km	Yes
Greystoke	Pub	Boot and Shoe	01768 483343	bootandshoegreystoke.co.uk	Yes	76km	Yes
Greystoke	B&B	Stafford House	01768 483558	stafford-house.co.uk	Nearby	76km	Yes
Greystoke	B&B	Beech House	01768 480829	beechhousegreystoke.co.uk	Nearby	76km	Yes
Newton Reigny	B&B/bunkhouse	Sun Inn	01768 867055	thesuninnnr.co.uk	Yes	82km	Yes
Newton Reigny	B&B	Sunset House	07500 367143	sunsethousebb.co.uk	Nearby	82km	Yes

Appendix A – Accommodation

Location	Type	Name	Phone	Website or email	Evening meal available	Distance along route	Bike storage
Penrith	Hostel	Wayfarers	01768 866011	wayfarershostel.com	Nearby	87km	Yes
Penrith	B&B	Norcroft Guesthouse	01768 862365	norcroft-guest-house.hotels-lake-district.com	Nearby	87km	Yes
Penrith	Camping	Crossfells Campsite	07551 339697	crossfells-campsite.co.uk		87km +4km	
Penrith	B&B	Acorn Guest House	01768 868696	acorn-guesthouse.co.uk	Nearby	87km	Yes
Penrith	B&B	Bank House	01768 868714	bankhousepenrith.co.uk	Nearby	87km	Yes
Penrith	Hotel	Station Hotel	01768 866714	stationpenrith.co.uk	Yes	87km	Yes
Penrith	B&B	Brooklands Guest House	01768 863395	brooklandsguesthouse.com	Nearby	87km	Yes
Langwathby	Pub	Shepherd's Inn	01768 881463	shepherds-inn.co.uk	Yes	95km	Yes
Little Salkeld	Camping and group accomm	Bank House Farm	01768 881257	edenvalleycampingandcaravans.com/	1 mile	98km	Yes
Alston	Pub	Angel Inn	01434 381363		Yes	123km +3km	
Alston	Hostel	Alston youth hostel	01434 381509	alstonyouthhostel.co.uk	Yes	123km +3km	Yes
Alston	Pub	The Cumberland Inn	01434 381875	cumberlandalston.co.uk	Yes	123km +3km	Yes
Alston	Hotel	Alston House Hotel	01434 382200	alstonhousehotel.co.uk	Yes	123km +3km	Yes

The Coast to Coast Cycle Route

Location	Type	Name	Phone	Website or email	Evening meal available	Distance along route	Bike storage
Alston	Camping	Tyne Willows	01434 382515			123km +3km	
Garrigill	B&B	East View	01434 381561		Nearby	124km	Yes
Garrigill	Camping, bunkhouse	Garrigill village hall	01434 647516	garrigillvh.org.uk	Nearby	124km	
Nenthead	Bunkhouse	Mill Cottage Bunkhouse	01434 381023	millcottagebunkhouse.com		130km	Yes
Nenthead	Bunkhouse	Assay House	07702 538709	nentheadmines.com		130km	
Nentsberry	Bunkhouse, camping	Haggs Bank	01434 382486	haggsbank.com	Yes for groups	128km +3km	Yes
Allenheads	Pub	The Allenheads Inn	01434 685200	allendheadsinn.co.uk	Yes	140km	Yes
Allenheads	B&B	Old School House	07966 257276		Nearby	140km	
Allenheads	B&B	Blacketts Retreat	01434 685260	allenheadsc2c.com	Nearby	140km	
Allenheads	Bunkhouse, camping	Thorn Green	01434 685234	thorngreenaccommodation.co.uk	1 mile	140km	Yes
Allenheads	Bunkhouse	Allenheads Lodge	01434 685374	springboard-ne.org.uk/morefromus	½ mile	140km	Yes
Rookhope	Bunkhouse	Barrington Bunkhouse	01388 517656	barrington-bunkhouse-rookhope.com		150km	Yes

118

Appendix A – Accommodation

Location	Type	Name	Phone	Website or email	Evening meal available	Distance along route	Bike storage
Eastgate	Pub	Cross Keys	01388 517234	crosskeyseastgate.co.uk	Yes	154km +4km	Yes
Eastgate	Bunkhouse	Hole House	01388 517311		At pub	154km +4km	Yes
Stanhope	Pub	Bonny Moorhen Hotel	01388 528877		Yes	157km	
Stanhope	Bunkhouse	Grey Bull	07885 676575		Nearby	157km	Yes
Stanhope	Self catering	Belle Vue Country	01388 526225	tranquil-life.info	1 mile	157km +1.5km	Yes
Stanhope	Pub/ B&B	Packhorse Inn	01388 528407	packhorsestanhope.co.uk	Nearby	157km	Yes
Stanhope	B&B	The Fossil Tree	01388 527851		Nearby	157km	
Stanhope/ Parkhead	B&B and bunk room	Parkhead Station	01388 526434	parkheadstation.co.uk	Yes	160km	Yes
Consett	B&B	Deneview	01207 502925	deneview.co.uk	Nearby	179km +1km	Yes
Consett	Camping	Manor Park	01207 501000		2.5 miles	179km +2km	
Greencroft	Camping	The Granary	02107 520842		1 mile	179km +2km	
Leadgate	B&B	High Brooms Granary	01207 500922	highbroomsgranary.co.uk	Nearby	180km	

THE COAST TO COAST CYCLE ROUTE

Location	Type	Name	Phone	Website or email	Evening meal available	Distance along route	Bike storage
Rowlands Gill	Camping	Derwent Park	01207 543383		Nearby	190km	
Newcastle	YHA hostel	Newcastle Central YHA	0345 260 2583	yha.org.uk	Yes	104km +1km	Yes
Tynemouth	B&B	Tynemouth 61	0191 2573687	no61.co.uk	Nearby	223km	
Tynemouth	Hotel	The Montagu Park Hotel	0191 2571406	parkhoteltynemouth.co.uk	Yes	223km	Yes
South Shields	B&B	Annie's Guest House	0191 456 6088	anniesguesthouse.co.uk		223km +2km	
South Shields	Hotel	The Little Haven Hotel	0191 455 4455	littlehavenhotel.com	Yes	223km +2km	
Stanley	B&B	The Ball Alley	01207 281577		Nearby	190km alt	
Beamish	Hotel	Beamish Mary Inn	0191 3920543	beamish-mary-inn.co.uk	Yes	193km alt	
Sunderland	B&B	Roker View	07801 089240		Nearby	216km alt	
Sunderland	B&B	Abbey Guesthouse	0191 514 0678		Nearby	216km alt	
Sunderland	B&B	The Lemonfield Hotel	0191 529 3018			216km alt	
Sunderland	B&B	April Guest House	0191 565 9550		Nearby	216km alt	

APPENDIX B
Bike shops and other useful contacts

Support companies

Cycle/baggage transport and getting to/from start/finish

Pedal Power (also offers packages)
tel 01665 713448 or 07790 596782
www.pedal-power.co.uk

Eco Cycle Adventures
tel 01434 600600
www.ecocycleadventures.co.uk

The Bike Bus Stanley Travel
tel 01207 237424
www.stanley-travel.com/the-bike-bus

Haven Cycles
tel 01946 63263
www.havencycles-c2cservices.co.uk

Sherpa Van
tel 01748 826917
www.sherpavan.com

Companies that arrange accommodation and transport as a package

Trailbrakes
tel 01416 286676 or 07922 653327
www.trailbrakes.co.uk

CycleActive
tel 01768 840400
www.cycleactive.com

Peak tours
tel 01457 851462
www.peak-tours.com

Skedaddle
tel 0191 2651110
www.skedaddle.com

Xplore
tel 01325 313609
www.xplorebritain.com

Macs Adventure
tel 0141 5305452
www.macsdaventure.com

Norcroft Guesthouse
tel 01768 862365
www.norcroft-guesthouse.co.uk

Bike shops (in route order)

Whitehaven

Haven Cycles
2 Preston Street
LA1 1NZ
tel 01946 63263
www.havencycles-c2cservices.co.uk

Workington

Halfords
Derwent Dr Retail Park
CA14 3YW
tel 01900 601635
www.halfords.com

Cleator Moor

Ainfield Cycles
Jacktrees Rd
CA23 3DW
tel 01946 812427
www.ainfieldcycles.co.uk

The Coast to Coast Cycle Route

Cockermouth

Cyclewise
Unit 2 Fairfield Buildings
(also based in Whinlatter Forest)
CA13 9RU
tel 01900 821998 or 01768 778711
www.cyclewise.co.uk

4Play Cycles
25–31 Market Place
CA13 9NH
tel 01900 823377
www.4playcycles.co.uk

Qwink
9 Vicarage Lane
CA13 9DG
tel 07447 642513
www.qwink.co.uk

Keswick

Bike Treks
133 Main St
CA12 5NJ
tel 01539 431245
www.bike-treks.co.uk

Whinlatter Bikes
82 Main Street
CA12 5DX
tel 01768 773940
www.whinlatterbikes.com

Penrith

Arragon's
2 Brunswick Rd
CA11 7LU
tel 01768 890344
www.arragons.com

Halfords
Unit 2 Castle Retail Park
tel 01768 892960
www.halfords.com

Nenthead

North Pennine Cycles
Nenthead
CA9 3PF
tel 01434 381324
www.northpenninecycles.co.uk

Consett

Bits4Bikes
2 John St Square
DH8 5AR
tel 01207 501188
www.bits4bikes.co.uk

Steel Town Cycles
Unit 4, 25–27 Derwent St
DH8 8RL
tel 01207 258270 or 07429421066
www.steeltowncycles.co.uk

Gateshead

Backyard Bike Shop
Hillgate Quay
NE8 2BH
tel 07519 098963
www.backyardbikeshop.com

Evans Cycles
Unit 2 Allison Court, Metrocentre
NE11 9YS
tel 0343 9092087
www.evanscycles.com

Newcastle

The Cycle Hub
Quayside
NE6 1BU
tel 0191 2767250
www.thecyclehub.org

Appendix B – Bike shops and other useful contacts

Start Cycles
Market St
NE1 6JE
tel 0191 9173803
www.startfitness.co.uk

North Shields

Tyne Cycles
19–20 Rudyerd St
NE29 6RR
tel 0191 2592266
www.tynecycles.co.uk

Tynemouth

Whiptail Cycles
3 Livingstone View
NE30 2PL
tel 0191 2572212
www.whiptail-cycles.co.uk

Sunderland

Cycleworld
222 High St W
Sunniside
SR1 1TZ
tel 0191 5141974 or 0191 5658188
www.cycleworldshop.co.uk

Darke Cycles
1 John St, Sunniside
SR1 1DX
tel 0191 5678310
www.darkecycles.co.uk

Climbing up from the dip at Coalcleugh (Stage 2)

DOWNLOAD THE ROUTES IN GPX FORMAT

All the routes in this guide are available for download from:

www.cicerone.co.uk/1118/GPX

as standard format GPX files. You should be able to load them into most online GPX systems and mobile devices, whether GPS or smartphone. You may need to convert the file into your preferred format using a conversion programme such as gpsvisualizer.com or one of the many other such websites and programmes.

When you follow this link, you will be asked for your email address and where you purchased the guidebook, and have the option to subscribe to the Cicerone e-newsletter.

www.cicerone.co.uk

LISTING OF CICERONE GUIDES

BRITISH ISLES CHALLENGES, COLLECTIONS AND ACTIVITIES
Cycling Land's End to John o' Groats
Great Walks on the England Coast Path
The Big Rounds
The Book of the Bivvy
The Book of the Bothy
The Mountains of England & Wales:
  Vol 1 Wales
  Vol 2 England
The National Trails
Walking the End to End Trail

SCOTLAND
Ben Nevis and Glen Coe
Cycle Touring in Northern Scotland
Cycling in the Hebrides
Great Mountain Days in Scotland
Mountain Biking in Southern and Central Scotland
Mountain Biking in West and North West Scotland
Not the West Highland Way Scotland
Scotland's Mountain Ridges
Scottish Wild Country Backpacking
Skye's Cuillin Ridge Traverse
The Borders Abbeys Way
The Great Glen Way
The Great Glen Way Map Booklet
The Hebridean Way
The Hebrides
The Isle of Mull
The Isle of Skye
The Skye Trail
The Southern Upland Way
The Speyside Way
The Speyside Way Map Booklet
The West Highland Way
The West Highland Way Map Booklet
Walking Ben Lawers, Rannoch and Atholl
Walking in the Cairngorms
Walking in the Pentland Hills
Walking in the Scottish Borders
Walking in the Southern Uplands
Walking in Torridon, Fisherfield, Fannichs and An Teallach
Walking Loch Lomond and the Trossachs
Walking on Arran
Walking on Harris and Lewis
Walking on Jura, Islay and Colonsay
Walking on Rum and the Small Isles
Walking on the Orkney and Shetland Isles
Walking on Uist and Barra
Walking the Cape Wrath Trail
Walking the Corbetts
  Vol 1 South of the Great Glen
  Vol 2 North of the Great Glen
Walking the Galloway Hills
Walking the John o' Groats Trail
Walking the Munros
  Vol 1 – Southern, Central and Western Highlands
  Vol 2 – Northern Highlands and the Cairngorms
Winter Climbs: Ben Nevis and Glen Coe

NORTHERN ENGLAND ROUTES
Cycling the Reivers Route
Cycling the Way of the Roses
Hadrian's Cycleway
Hadrian's Wall Path
Hadrian's Wall Path Map Booklet
Short Walks Hadrian's Wall
The Coast to Coast Cycle Route
The Coast to Coast Walk
The Coast to Coast Map Booklet
The Pennine Way
The Pennine Way Map Booklet
Walking the Dales Way
Walking the Dales Way Map Booklet

NORTH-EAST ENGLAND, YORKSHIRE DALES AND PENNINES
Cycling in the Yorkshire Dales
Great Mountain Days in the Pennines
Mountain Biking in the Yorkshire Dales
St Oswald's Way and St Cuthbert's Way
The Cleveland Way and the Yorkshire Wolds Way
The Cleveland Way Map Booklet
The North York Moors
The Reivers Way
Trail and Fell Running in the Yorkshire Dales
Walking in County Durham
Walking in Northumberland
Walking in the North Pennines
Walking in the Yorkshire Dales:
  North and East
  South and West

NORTH-WEST ENGLAND AND THE ISLE OF MAN
Cycling the Pennine Bridleway
Isle of Man Coastal Path
Short Walks in Arnside and Silverdale
The Lancashire Cycleway
The Lune Valley and Howgills
Walking in Cumbria's Eden Valley
Walking in Lancashire
Walking in the Forest of Bowland and Pendle
Walking on the Isle of Man
Walking on the West Pennine Moors
Walks in Silverdale and Arnside

LAKE DISTRICT
Cycling in the Lake District
Great Mountain Days in the Lake District
Joss Naylor's Lakes, Meres and Waters of the Lake District
Lake District Winter Climbs
Lake District: High Level and Fell Walks
Lake District: Low Level and Lake Walks
Mountain Biking in the Lake District
Outdoor Adventures with Children – Lake District
Scrambles in the Lake District – North
Scrambles in the Lake District – South
Short Walks in the Lake District: Windermere Ambleside and Grasmere
Trail and Fell Running in the Lake District
Walking The Cumbria Way
Walking the Lake District Fells:
  Borrowdale
  Buttermere
  Coniston
  Keswick
  Langdale
  Mardale and the Far East
  Patterdale
  Wasdale
Walking the Tour of the Lake District

DERBYSHIRE, PEAK DISTRICT AND MIDLANDS
Cycling in the Peak District
Dark Peak Walks
Scrambles in the Dark Peak
Walking in Derbyshire
Walking in the Peak District – White Peak East
Walking in the Peak District – White Peak West

SOUTHERN ENGLAND
20 Classic Sportive Rides in South East England
20 Classic Sportive Rides in South West England
Cycling in the Cotswolds

Mountain Biking on the North Downs
Mountain Biking on the South Downs
Short Walks in the Surrey Hills
Suffolk Coast and Heath Walks
The Cotswold Way
The Cotswold Way Map Booklet
The Kennet and Avon Canal
The Lea Valley Walk
The North Downs Way
The North Downs Way Map Booklet
The Peddars Way and Norfolk Coast Path
The Pilgrims' Way
The Ridgeway National Trail
The Ridgeway Map Booklet
The South Downs Way
The South Downs Way Map Booklet
The Thames Path
The Thames Path Map Booklet
The Two Moors Way
The Two Moors Way Map Booklet
Walking Hampshire's Test Way
Walking in Cornwall
Walking in Essex
Walking in Kent
Walking in London
Walking in Norfolk
Walking in the Chilterns
Walking in the Cotswolds
Walking in the Isles of Scilly
Walking in the New Forest
Walking in the North Wessex Downs
Walking on Guernsey
Walking on Jersey
Walking on the Isle of Wight
Walking the Jurassic Coast
Walking the South West Coast Path
Walking the South West Coast Path Map Booklets:
Vol 1: Minehead to St Ives
Vol 2: St Ives to Plymouth
Vol 3: Plymouth to Poole
Walks in the South Downs National Park

WALES AND WELSH BORDERS

Cycle Touring in Wales
Cycling Lon Las Cymru
Glyndwr's Way
Great Mountain Days in Snowdonia
Hillwalking in Shropshire
Hillwalking in Wales – Vols 1&2
Mountain Walking in Snowdonia
Offa's Dyke Path
Offa's Dyke Map Booklet
Ridges of Snowdonia
Scrambles in Snowdonia
Snowdonia: 30 Low-level and Easy Walks – North
Snowdonia: 30 Low-level and Easy Walks – South
The Cambrian Way
The Pembrokeshire Coast Path
The Pembrokeshire Coast Path Map Booklet
The Severn Way
The Snowdonia Way
The Wye Valley Walk
Walking in Carmarthenshire
Walking in Pembrokeshire
Walking in the Brecon Beacons
Walking in the Forest of Dean
Walking in the Wye Valley
Walking on Gower
Walking the Shropshire Way
Walking the Wales Coast Path

INTERNATIONAL CHALLENGES, COLLECTIONS AND ACTIVITIES

Europe's High Points
Walking the Via Francigena Pilgrim Route – Part 1

AFRICA

Kilimanjaro
Walks and Scrambles in the Moroccan Anti-Atlas
Walking in the Drakensberg

ALPS CROSS-BORDER ROUTES

100 Hut Walks in the Alps
Alpine Ski Mountaineering
Vol 1 – Western Alps
Vol 2 – Central and Eastern Alps
The Karnischer Hohenweg
The Tour of the Bernina
Trail Running – Chamonix and the Mont Blanc region
Trekking Chamonix to Zermatt
Trekking in the Alps
Trekking in the Silvretta and Ratikon Alps
Trekking Munich to Venice
Trekking the Tour of Mont Blanc
Walking in the Alps

PYRENEES AND FRANCE/SPAIN CROSS-BORDER ROUTES

Shorter Treks in the Pyrenees
The GR10 Trail
The GR11 Trail
The Pyrenean Haute Route
The Pyrenees
Walks and Climbs in the Pyrenees

AUSTRIA

Innsbruck Mountain Adventures
Trekking in Austria's Hohe Tauern
Trekking in Austria's Zillertal Alps
Trekking in the Stubai Alps
Walking in Austria
Walking in the Salzkammergut: the Austrian Lake District

EASTERN EUROPE

The Danube Cycleway Vol 2
The Elbe Cycle Route
The High Tatras
The Mountains of Romania
Walking in Bulgaria's National Parks
Walking in Hungary

FRANCE, BELGIUM AND LUXEMBOURG

Camino de Santiago – Via Podiensis
Chamonix Mountain Adventures
Cycle Touring in France
Cycling London to Paris
Cycling the Canal de la Garonne
Cycling the Canal du Midi
Cycling the Route des Grandes Alpes
Mont Blanc Walks
Mountain Adventures in the Maurienne
Short Treks on Corsica
The GR5 Trail
The GR5 Trail – Benelux and Lorraine
The GR5 Trail – Vosges and Jura
The Grand Traverse of the Massif Central
The Moselle Cycle Route
The River Loire Cycle Route
The River Rhone Cycle Route
Trekking in the Vanoise
Trekking the Cathar Way
Trekking the GR20 Corsica
Trekking the Robert Louis Stevenson Trail
Via Ferratas of the French Alps
Walking in Provence – East
Walking in Provence – West
Walking in the Ardennes
Walking in the Auvergne
Walking in the Briançonnais
Walking in the Dordogne
Walking in the Haute Savoie: North
Walking in the Haute Savoie: South
Walking on Corsica
Walking the Brittany Coast Path

GERMANY

Hiking and Cycling in the Black Forest
The Danube Cycleway Vol 1
The Rhine Cycle Route
The Westweg
Walking in the Bavarian Alps

IRELAND

The Wild Atlantic Way and Western Ireland
Walking the Wicklow Way

ITALY
- Alta Via 1 – Trekking in the Dolomites
- Alta Via 2 – Trekking in the Dolomites
- Italy's Sibillini National Park
- Shorter Walks in the Dolomites
- Ski Touring and Snowshoeing in the Dolomites
- The Way of St Francis
- Trekking in the Apennines
- Trekking the Giants' Trail: Alta Via 1 through the Italian Pennine Alps
- Via Ferratas of the Italian Dolomites Vols 1&2
- Walking and Trekking in the Gran Paradiso
- Walking in Abruzzo
- Walking in Italy's Cinque Terre
- Walking in Italy's Stelvio National Park
- Walking in Sicily
- Walking in the Aosta Valley
- Walking in the Dolomites
- Walking in Tuscany
- Walking in Umbria
- Walking Lake Como and Maggiore
- Walking Lake Garda and Iseo
- Walking on the Amalfi Coast
- Walking the Via Francigena Pilgrim Route – Part 2
- Pilgrim Route – Part 3
- Walks and Treks in the Maritime Alps

MEDITERRANEAN
- The High Mountains of Crete
- Trekking in Greece
- Walking and Trekking in Zagori
- Walking and Trekking on Corfu
- Walking in Cyprus
- Walking on Malta
- Walking on the Greek Islands – the Cyclades

NEW ZEALAND AND AUSTRALIA
- Hiking the Overland Track

NORTH AMERICA
- Hiking and Cycling the California Missions Trail
- The John Muir Trail
- The Pacific Crest Trail

SOUTH AMERICA
- Aconcagua and the Southern Andes
- Hiking and Biking Peru's Inca Trails
- Torres del Paine

SCANDINAVIA, ICELAND AND GREENLAND
- Hiking in Norway – South
- Trekking in Greenland – The Arctic Circle Trail
- Trekking the Kungsleden
- Walking and Trekking in Iceland

SLOVENIA, CROATIA, SERBIA, MONTENEGRO AND ALBANIA
- Mountain Biking in Slovenia
- The Islands of Croatia
- The Julian Alps of Slovenia
- The Mountains of Montenegro
- The Peaks of the Balkans Trail
- The Slovene Mountain Trail
- Walking in Slovenia: The Karavanke
- Walks and Treks in Croatia

SPAIN AND PORTUGAL
- Camino de Santiago: Camino Frances
- Coastal Walks in Andalucia
- Costa Blanca Mountain Adventures
- Cycling the Camino de Santiago
- Cycling the Ruta Via de la Plata
- Mountain Walking in Mallorca
- Mountain Walking in Southern Catalunya
- Portugal's Rota Vicentina
- Spain's Sendero Historico: The GR1
- The Andalucian Coast to Coast Walk
- The Camino del Norte and Camino Primitivo
- The Camino Ingles and Ruta do Mar
- The Camino Portugues
- The Mountains of Nerja
- The Mountains of Ronda and Grazalema
- The Sierras of Extremadura
- Trekking in Mallorca
- Trekking in the Canary Islands
- Trekking the GR7 in Andalucia
- Walking and Trekking in the Sierra Nevada
- Walking in Andalucia
- Walking in Catalunya – Barcelona
- Walking in Portugal
- Walking in the Algarve
- Walking on Gran Canaria
- Walking on La Gomera and El Hierro
- Walking on La Palma
- Walking on Lanzarote and Fuerteventura
- Walking on Madeira
- Walking on Tenerife
- Walking on the Azores
- Walking on the Costa Blanca
- Walking the Camino dos Faros

SWITZERLAND
- Switzerland's Jura Crest Trail
- The Swiss Alps
- Tour of the Jungfrau Region
- Walking in the Bernese Oberland
- Walking in the Engadine – Switzerland
- Walking in the Valais
- Walking in Ticino
- Walking in Zermatt and Saas-Fee

CHINA, JAPAN AND ASIA
- Hiking and Trekking in the Japan Alps and Mount Fuji
- Hiking in Hong Kong
- Japan's Kumano Kodo Pilgrimage
- Trekking in Tajikistan

HIMALAYA
- Annapurna
- Everest: A Trekker's Guide
- Trekking in Bhutan
- Trekking in Ladakh
- Trekking in the Himalaya

MOUNTAIN LITERATURE
- 8000 metres
- A Walk in the Clouds
- Abode of the Gods
- Fifty Years of Adventure
- The Pennine Way – the Path, the People, the Journey
- Unjustifiable Risk?

TECHNIQUES
- Fastpacking
- Geocaching in the UK
- Map and Compass
- Outdoor Photography
- Polar Exploration
- The Mountain Hut Book

MINI GUIDES
- Alpine Flowers
- Navigation
- Pocket First Aid and Wilderness Medicine
- Snow

For full information on all our guides, books and eBooks, visit our website:
www.cicerone.co.uk

CICERONE

Trust Cicerone to guide your next adventure, wherever it may be around the world...

Discover guides for hiking, mountain walking, backpacking, trekking, trail running, cycling and mountain biking, ski touring, climbing and scrambling in Britain, Europe and worldwide.

Connect with Cicerone online and find inspiration.

- buy books and ebooks
- articles, advice and trip reports
- podcasts and live events
- GPX files and updates
- regular newsletter

cicerone.co.uk